P9-DTY-030

LOOK, MA, I AM KOOL!
And Other Casuals

Other Books by Burton Bernstein

The Grove
The Lost Art
The Sticks
Thurber: A Biography

LOOK, MA, I AM KOOL!
And Other Casuals

(Being a collection of humor pieces by
youngish writers, in which the question
"Whatever happened to literate humor?"
is, perhaps, answered)

Compiled and Edited by Burton Bernstein

PRENTICE-HALL, INC., Englewood Cliffs, N. J.

For Candida Donadio

Look, Ma, I Am Kool! And Other Casuals, Compiled and Edited
by Burton Bernstein
Copyright © 1977 by Burton Bernstein
All rights reserved. No part of this book may be
reproduced in any form or by any means, except
for the inclusion of brief quotations in a review,
without permission in writing from the publisher.
Printed in the United States of America
Prentice-Hall International, Inc., London
Prentice-Hall of Australia, Pty. Ltd., Sydney
Prentice-Hall of Canada, Ltd., Toronto
Prentice-Hall of India Private Ltd., New Delhi
Prentice-Hall of Japan, Inc., Tokyo
Prentice-Hall of Southeast Asia Pte. Ltd., Singapore
Whitehall Books Ltd., Wellington, New Zealand

10 9 8 7 6 5 4 3 2 1

Library of Congress Cataloging in Publication Data
Main entry under title:
Look, ma, I am kool! and other casuals.
    1. American wit and humor. I. Bernstein, Burton.
PN6162.L585 817'.008—76-51777
ISBN 0-13-540575-0

Contents

Foreword

When *Thurber*, my biography of James Thurber, was issued in early 1975, the publisher sent me on one of those television-radio-bookstore promotional tours through a goodly part of the United States and Canada. In city after city, interviewers would ask the expected pertinent questions ("What was James Thurber *really* like?" and "Why do American writers drink so much?"), and then, invariably, somebody would wonder whether there was a present or a future for literate American humor, after the passing of Thurber, Robert Benchley, Ring Lardner, H. L. Mencken, Dorothy Parker, and most of the old guard. My practiced reply, invariably, was that literate American humor is alive and well but harder to find, that's all. Eyes narrowing in disbelief, the interviewers would press on to other pertinent questions ("What is Brendan Gill *really* like?" and "Can you move a little closer to the microphone, please?"). The crucial question "Whatever happened to literate humor?" continued to hang darkly in the air, and I decided that a more satisfying answer was called for. This book is an attempt at such an answer.

Literate humor has traditionally been at its best, it seems to me, in its short form, which *New Yorker* editors call the "casual." Aptly named, the casual is a seemingly offhand kind of work, constructed with such cunning that it appears to have been born whole, effortlessly and spontaneously—what the Italians call *sprezzatura*. The reader should suspect that the writer, while, say, brushing his teeth one morning, was visited by afflatus and, after a quick stop at his typewriter, was blessed with the finished article before his first cup of coffee was consumed. Its actual process of creation, of course, is precisely the opposite. The casual is one of the more difficult and painstaking forms of writing known to humankind. In fact, it is often sheer hell to get one down on paper, let alone accepted for publication. Every contributor to this book will attest to that.

The categories of casuals are as numerous as are the categories of satire, which is what all effective humor is, fundamentally. (Humorists worthy of the title must make some sort of moral point in order to face themselves in the mirror each morning, and making a moral point is the function of satire.) There is the basic situation casual, in which a symptom of the human condition is manhandled until its inborn ridiculousness is carried to impossible extremes. There is the time-honored essay casual—a favorite of E. B. White, America's greatest living essayist—in which a case for or against an issue is simply stated, using humor as the sly persuader. There is the first-person reminiscence casual —Thurber's favorite—in which a bud of past truth becomes a flamboyant fictional flower. There is the parody casual, ideally not a photographic facsimile, as in a burlesque or lampoon, but rather a telling reflection that projects the subject to an absurd next stage...leading to the nonsense casual—so comfortably combined with other casual species—in which the delightfully insane device of nonsense is employed in order to lend some sanity to life. Then there are the fantasy casual (the writer's imagination irresponsibly letting go), the character casual (practically a short story concerning a fictional person, quite often a version of the author), and the word-game casual (designed for the peculiar creature who "sees words dancing in his head," as Mark Van Doren once described Thurber)—and, of course, various combinations of all these categories.

Once upon a time, literate humor was just about all that made America laugh. In the nineteenth century, when literate humor was rolling across the land, Mark Twain could boast that the publication of one of his first short pieces, "The Celebrated Jumping Frog of Calaveras County," made him widely known in three continents and earned him tens of thousands of dollars. And he had a lot of company then—people with such names as Petroleum V. Nasby, Josh Billings, Artemus Ward, George Ade, and Finley Peter Dunne. Yet, of them all, only Twain survived as a pillar of American literature, because Twain was a truly *literate* humorist. As he said in his autobiography: "Humor must not professedly teach and must not professedly preach, but it must do both if it would live forever." (And by "forever," he added, "I mean thirty years.")

What made Twain's humor so literate and lasting, besides the monumental writing talent it demonstrated, was his dedication to an apparently light and frivolous craft for, as Twain put it, the "deriding of sham, the exposure of pretentious falsities, the laughing of stupid superstitions out of existence." Through the use of humor, he declared war on pomposity and its "kindred swindles" and befriended the causes of justice and human liberty. "Against the assault of laughter nothing can stand," Twain was to write—a sentiment echoed by Thurber a half-century later when he said, apropos of McCarthyism, "When a democracy begins to laugh at boogie men, it is no longer in danger of destroying itself." E. B. White put it most succinctly when he wrote that effective humor "need only speak the truth." The literate humorist satirizes, parodies, punctures, and deflates anything and everything he sees as a threat to logic and sanity.

With Twain as the spiritual and sometimes physical model, literate humorists founded a new golden age in the post-World War I era of high times and plenty. There was no end of subjects ripe for ridicule then, and there were outlets galore—*Vanity Fair, Smart Set, Harper's, Life, Puck, Judge,* and dozens of newspaper catchall columns, like Franklin P. Adams's "The Conning Tower." Then, in 1925, along came an upstart magazine that promised to deliver to the literate world the ultimate in sophisticated humor—*The New Yorker*, not designed, as it proclaimed in its prospectus, for the little old lady in Dubuque. It had some difficulty living up to that tall order at first, but with the arrival in its cramped, shoddy offices of such writers as White, Thurber, Benchley, Parker, Russell Maloney, John McNulty, S. J. Perelman, Wolcott Gibbs, and Frank Sullivan, *The New Yorker* began to fit its own immodest description of itself, for these writers had perfected the ultimate weapon in literate humor—the casual.

Everything went swimmingly until the 1950's and the rise of something called television. Soon, it seemed that the American public wasn't able to distinguish between a humorist and a comedian; it was far easier to watch than to read (it still is), and the remaining magazines that occasionally published humor began to drop like Apaches on the magic tube that did them in. To all intents and purposes, there was only *The New Yorker* as a regular, dependable outlet for literate humor. Meanwhile, Benchley had died. So had Lardner and Maloney. McNulty and Gibbs were in their last days. White, Sullivan, and Parker went into semiretirement. Thurber became totally blind and totally bitter and almost totally unfunny. Only Perelman went on writing as before. One result of this depressing state of affairs was a concentration on straight factual reportage in that last outpost of literate humor.

However, inevitably, a new generation appeared—younger writers who stubbornly wanted to write humor in more or less the traditional fashion (often improving on the traditional fashion), in spite of the odds against them. Many of these writers, some now more youngish than young, would like to earn the major part of their incomes by creating casuals, but no longer do editors hunger for their output, as they did decades ago; Woody Allen, for instance, was reported by *Newsweek* to prefer writing humorous prose to making humorous movies. Nobody these days can make a decent living solely by writing humor, as Thurber and Benchley once did. Yet, the youngish humorists persist, and the *New Yorker* and a few valiant literate magazines still print casuals. (Only twenty-five percent of the pieces included in this anthology have been previously printed in *The New Yorker*, not out of the anthologist's choice but because of the magazine's limiting rule for unofficial collections.) With any luck, matters won't get worse and literate humor will remain alive and—if not exactly well—at least sitting up and taking nourishment. For many good people, there is something special and satisfying about literate humor, something you can't extract from television or radio or movies or theatre. It is the astonishing miracle of response the printed word alone can stir, and humor is a precious part of that miracle.

This book is, granted, a subjective, not definitive, collection of humor pieces. It was meant to include the work of only youngish casual writers; thus, there are no pieces herein by Thurber, White, Benchley, Parker, Twain, Lardner, Perelman, and others of the old guard. E. B. and Katharine S. White definitively collected those masters in their *A Subtreasury of American Humor*, first published in 1941. Rather, this collection, one hopes, will take up where the Whites left off, as an entertaining reminder that all is not lost, that literate humor is still a living form of literature.

If the emphasis is heavy on parody, it is due to the fact that wild parody is a particularly favored form of satire in these days when straight news stories seem to be wild parodies of themselves. But all the species of casuals mentioned above are represented here.

I have taken the traditional prerogative of the anthologist to include as many of my own pieces as I could possibly get away with. As Mark Twain wrote at the beginning of his *Library of Humor* anthology: "Those selections in this book which are from my own works were made by my two assistant compilers, not by me. This is why there are not more."

I want to thank all the contributors and their various publishers for their reprint permissions, as well as Walter Bernstein, Candida Donadio, Milton Greenstein, Peter Grenquist, P. J. O'Rourke, Helen Stark and her staff at *The New Yorker*'s library, and Robert Stewart.

Burton Bernstein
Bridgewater, Connecticut

LOOK, MA, I AM KOOL!
And Other Casuals

WOODY ALLEN

The Scrolls

Copyright © 1974 by Woody Allen. Reprinted from WITHOUT
FEATHERS, by Woody Allen, by permission of Random
House, Inc.
Reprinted by permission of *The New Republic.* © 1975 The
New Republic, Inc.

Scholars will recall that several years ago a shepherd,
wandering in the Gulf of Aqaba, stumbled upon a cave
containing several large clay jars and also two tickets to
the ice show. Inside the jars were discovered six parch-
ment scrolls with ancient incomprehensible writing
which the shepherd, in his ignorance, sold to the museum
for $750,000 apiece. Two years later the jars turned up in
a pawnshop in Philadelphia. One year later the shepherd
turned up in a pawnshop in Philadelphia and neither
was claimed.

Archaeologists originally set the date of the scrolls

at 4000 B.C., or just after the massacre of the Israelites by their benefactors. The writing is a mixture of Sumerian, Aramaic, and Babylonian and seems to have been done by either one man over a long period of time, or several men who shared the same suit. The authenticity of the scrolls is currently in great doubt, particularly since the word "Oldsmobile" appears several times in the text, and the few fragments that have finally been translated deal with familiar religious themes in a more than dubious way. Still, excavationist A. H. Bauer has noted that even though the fragments seem totally fraudulent, this is probably the greatest archeological find in history with the exception of the recovery of his cuff links from a tomb in Jerusalem. The following are the translated fragments.

One... And the Lord made an bet with Satan to test Job's loyalty and the Lord, for no apparent reason to Job, smote him on the head and again on the ear and pushed him into an thick sauce so as to make Job sticky and vile and then He slew a tenth part of Job's kine and Job calleth out: "Why doth thou slay my kine? Kine are hard to come by. Now I am short kine and I'm not even sure what kine are." And the Lord produced two stone tablets and snapped them closed on Job's nose. And when Job's wife saw this she wept and the Lord sent an angel of mercy who anointed her head with a polo mallet and of the ten plagues, the Lord sent one through six, inclusive, and Job was sore and his wife angry and she rent her garment and then raised the rent but refused to paint.

And soon Job's pastures dried up and his tongue cleaved to the roof of his mouth so he could not pronounce the word "frankincense" without getting big laughs.

And once the Lord, while wreaking havoc upon his faithful servant, came too close and Job grabbed him around the neck and said, "Aha! Now I got you! Why art thou giving Job a hard time, eh? Eh? Speak up!"

And the Lord said, "Er, look—that's my neck you have...Could you let me go?"

But Job showed no mercy and said, "I was doing very well till you came along. I had myrrh and fig trees in abundance and a coat of many colors with two pairs of pants of many colors. Now look."

And the Lord spake and his voice thundered: "Must I who created heaven and earth explain my ways to thee? What hath thou created that thou doth dare question me?"

"That's no answer," Job said. "And for someone who's supposed to be omnipotent, let me tell you, 'tabernacle' has only one *l*." Then Job fell to his knees and cried to the Lord, "Thine is the kingdom and the power and glory. Thou hast a good job. Don't blow it."

*Two...*And Abraham awoke in the middle of the night and said to his only son, Isaac, "I have had an dream where the voice of the Lord sayeth that I must sacrifice my only son, so put your pants on." And Isaac trembled and said, "So what did you say? I mean when He brought this whole thing up?"

"What am I going to say?" Abraham said. "I'm standing there at two A.M. in my underwear with the Creator of the Universe. Should I argue?"

"Well, did he say why he wants me sacrificed?" Isaac asked his father.

But Abraham said, "The faithful do not question. Now let's go because I have a heavy day tomorrow."

And Sarah who heard Abraham's plan grew vexed and said, "How doth thou know it was the Lord and not, say, thy friend who loveth practical jokes, for the Lord hateth practical jokes and whosoever shall pull one shall be delivered into the hands of his enemies whether they can pay the delivery charge or not." And Abraham answered, "Because I know it was the Lord. It was a deep, resonant voice, well modulated, and nobody in the desert can get a rumble in it like that."

And Sarah said, "And thou art willing to carry out this senseless act?" But Abraham told her, "Frankly yes, for to question the Lord's word is one of the worst things a person can do, particularly with the economy in the state it's in."

And so he took Isaac to a certain place and prepared to sacrifice him but at the last minute the Lord stayed Abraham's hand and said, "How could thou doest such a thing?"

And Abraham said, "But thou said—"

"Never mind what I said," the Lord spake. "Doth thou listen to every crazy idea that comes thy way?" And Abraham grew ashamed. "Er—not really...no."

"I jokingly suggest thou sacrifice Isaac and thou immediately runs out to do it."

And Abraham fell to his knees, "See, I never know when you're kidding."

And the Lord thundered, "No sense of humor. I can't believe it."

"But doth this not prove I love thee, that I was willing to donate mine only son on thy whim?"

And the Lord said, "It proves that some men will follow any order no matter how asinine as long as it comes from a resonant, well-modulated voice."

And with that, the Lord bid Abraham get some rest and check with him tomorrow.

*Three...*And it came to pass that a man who sold shirts was smitten by hard times. Neither did any of his merchandise move nor did he prosper. And he prayed and said, "Lord, why hast thou left me to suffer thus? All mine enemies sell their goods except I. And it's the height of the season. My shirts are good shirts. Take a look at this rayon. I got button-downs, flare collars, nothing sells. Yet I have kept thy commandments. Why can I not earn a living when mine younger brother cleans up in children's ready-to-wear?"

And the Lord heard the man and said, "About thy shirts..."

"Yes, Lord," the man said, falling to his knees.

"Put an alligator over the pocket."

"Pardon me, Lord?"

"Just do what I'm telling you. You won't be sorry."

And the man sewed on to all his shirts a small alligator symbol and lo and behold, suddenly his merchandise moved like gangbusters, and there was much rejoicing while amongst his enemies there was wailing and gnashing of teeth, and one said, "The Lord is merciful. He maketh me to lie down in green pastures. The problem is, I can't get up."

LAWS AND PROVERBS

Doing abominations is against the law, particularly if the abominations are done while wearing a lobster bib.

The lion and the calf shall lie down together but the calf won't get much sleep.

Whosoever shall not fall by the sword or by famine, shall fall by pestilence so why bother shaving?

The wicked at heart probably know something.

Whosoever loveth wisdom is righteous but he that keepeth company with fowl is weird.

My Lord, my Lord! What hast Thou done, lately?

The Irish Genius

Copyright © 1975 by Woody Allen. Reprinted from WITHOUT
FEATHERS, by Woody Allen, by permission of Random
House, Inc.
Reprinted by permission of The New Republic. © 1975
The New Republic, Inc.

Viscous and Sons has announced publication of *The Annotated Poems of Sean O'Shawn*, the great Irish poet, considered by many to be the most incomprehensible and hence the finest poet of his time. Abounding in highly personal references, any understanding of O'Shawn's work requires an intimate knowledge of his life, which, according to scholars, not even he had.

Following is a sample from this fine book.

BEYOND ICHOR

Let us sail. Sail with
Fogarty's chin to Alexandria,
While the Beamish Brothers
Hurry giggling to the tower,

WOODY ALLEN

Proud of their gums.
A thousand years passed since
Agamemnon said, "Don't open
The gates, who the hell needs
A wooden horse that size?"
What is the connection? Only
That Shaunnesy, with dying
Breath, refused to order an
Appetizer with his meal although
He was entitled to it.
And brave Bixby, despite his
Resemblance to a woodpecker,
Could not retrieve his underwear
From Socrates without a ticket.

Parnell had the answer, but no
One would ask him the question.
No one but old Lafferty, whose
Lapis lazuli practical joke caused
A whole generation to take
Samba lessons.
True, Homer was blind and that
Accounted for why he dated those
Particular women.
But Aegnus and the Druids bear
Mute testimony to man's quest
For free alterations.
Blake dreamed of it too, and
O'Higgins who had his suit
Stolen while he was still in it.
Civilization is shaped like a
Circle and repeats itself, while
O'Leary's head is shaped like
A trapezoid.
Rejoice! Rejoice! And call your
Mother once in a while.

Let us sail. O'Shawn was fond of sailing, although he had never done it on the sea. As a boy he dreamed of becoming a ship's captain but gave it up when someone explained to him what sharks were. His older brother James, however, did go off and join the British Navy, though he was dishonorably discharged for selling coleslaw to a bosun.

Fogarty's chin. Undoubtedly a reference to George Fogarty, who convinced O'Shawn to become a poet and assured him he would still be invited to parties. Fogarty published a magazine for new poets and although its circulation was limited to his mother, its impact was international.

Fogarty was a fun-loving, rubicund Irishman whose idea of a good time was to lie down in the public square and imitate a tweezers. Eventually he suffered a nervous breakdown and was arrested for eating a pair of pants on Good Friday.

Fogarty's chin was an object of great ridicule because it was tiny to the point of nonexistence, and at Jim Kelly's wake, he told O'Shawn, "I'd give anything for a larger chin. If I don't find one soon I'm liable to do something rash." Fogarty, incidentally, was a friend of Bernard Shaw's and was once permitted to touch Shaw's beard, provided he would go away.

Alexandria. References to the Middle East appear throughout O'Shawn's work, and his poem that begins "To Bethlehem with suds..." deals caustically with the hotel business seen through the eyes of a mummy.

The Beamish Brothers. Two half-wit brothers who tried to get from Belfast to Scotland by mailing each other.

Liam Beamish went to Jesuit school with O'Shawn but was thrown out for dressing like a beaver. Quincy Beamish was the more introverted of the two and kept a furniture pad on his head till he was forty-one.

The Beamish Brothers used to pick on O'Shawn and usually ate his lunch just before he did. Still, O'Shawn remembers them fondly and in his best sonnet, "My love is like a great, great yak," they appear symbolically as end tables.

The tower. When O'Shawn moved out of his parents' home, he lived in a tower just south of Dublin. It was a very low tower, standing about six feet, or two inches shorter than O'Shawn. He shared this residence with Harry O'Connel, a friend with literary pretensions, whose verse play *The Musk Ox* closed abruptly when the cast was chloroformed.

O'Connel was a great influence on O'Shawn's style and ultimately convinced him that every poem need not begin, "Roses are red, violets are blue."

Proud of their gums. The Beamish Brothers had unusually fine gums. Liam Beamish could remove his false teeth and eat peanut brittle, which he did every day for sixteen years until someone told him there was no such profession.

Agamemnon. O'Shawn was obsessed with the Trojan War. He could not believe an army could be so stupid as to accept a gift from its enemy during wartime. Particularly when they got close to the wooden horse and heard giggling inside. This episode seems to have traumatized the young O'Shawn and throughout his entire life he examined every gift given him very carefully, going so far as to shine a flashlight into a pair of shoes he received on his birthday and calling out, "Anybody in there? Eh? Come on out!"

Shaunnesy. Michael Shaunnesy, an occult writer and mystic, who convinced O'Shawn there would be a life after death for those who saved string.

Shaunnesy also believed the moon influenced actions and that to take a haircut during a total eclipse caused sterility. O'Shawn was very much taken with Shaunnesy and devoted much of his life to occult studies, although he never achieved his final goal of being able to enter a room through the keyhole.

The moon figures heavily in O'Shawn's later poems, and he told James Joyce that one of his greatest pleasures was to immerse his arm in custard on a moonlit night.

The reference to Shaunnesy's refusing an appetizer probably refers to the time the two men dined together in Innesfree and Shaunnesy blew chickpeas through a straw at a fat lady when she disagreed with his views on embalming.

Bixby. Eamon Bixby. A political fanantic who preached ventriloquism as a cure for the world's ills. He was a great student of Socrates but differed from the Greek philosopher in his idea of the "good life," which Bixby felt was impossible unless everybody weighed the same.

Parnell had the answer. The answer O'Shawn refers to is "Tin," and the question is "What is the chief export of Bolivia?" That no one asked Parnell the question is understandable, although he was challenged once to name the largest fur-bearing quadruped extant and he said, "Chicken," for which he was severely criticized.

Lafferty. John Millington Synge's podiatrist. A fascinating character who had a passionate affair with Molly Bloom until he realized she was a fictional character.

Lafferty was fond of practical jokes, and once with some corn meal and egg, he breaded Synge's arch supports. Synge walked peculiarly as a result, and his followers imitated him, hoping that by duplicating his gait, they too would write fine plays. Hence the lines: "caused/A whole generation to take/Samba lessons."

Homer was blind. Homer was a symbol for T. S. Eliot, whom O'Shawn considered a poet of "immense scope but very little breadth."

The two men met in London at rehearsals of *Murder in the Cathedral* (at that time entitled *Million Dollar Legs*). O'Shawn persuaded Eliot to abandon his sideburns and give up any notion he might have of becoming a Spanish dancer. Both writers then composed a manifesto stating the aims of the "new poetry," one of which was to write fewer poems that dealt with rabbits.

Aegnus and the Druids. O'Shawn was influenced by Celtic mythology, and his poem that begins, "Clooth na bare, na bare, na bare..." tells how the gods of ancient Ireland transformed two lovers into a set of the Encyclopaedia Britannica.

Free alterations. Probably refers to O'Shawn's wish to "alter the human race," whom he felt were basically depraved, especially jockeys. O'Shawn was definitely a pessimist and felt that no good could come of mankind until they agreed to lower their body temperature from 98.6, which he felt was unreasonable.

Blake. O'Shawn was a mystic and, like Blake, believed in unseen forces. This was confirmed for him when his brother Ben was struck by lightning while licking a postage stamp. The lightning failed to kill Ben, which O'Shawn attributed to Providence, although it took his brother seventeen years before he could get his tongue back in his mouth.

O'Higgins. Patrick O'Higgins introduced O'Shawn to Polly Flaherty, who was to become O'Shawn's wife after a courtship of ten years in which the two did nothing more than meet secretly and wheeze at each other. Polly never realized the extent of her husband's genius and told intimates she thought he would be most remembered not for his poetry but for his habit of emitting a piercing shriek just before eating apples.

O'Leary's head. Mount O'Leary, where O'Shawn proposed to Polly just before she rolled off. O'Shawn visited her in the hospital and won her heart with his poem "On the Decomposing of Flesh."

Call your mother. On her deathbed, O'Shawn's mother, Bridget, begged her son to abandon poetry and become a vacuum-cleaner salesman. O'Shawn couldn't promise and suffered from anxiety and guilt the rest of his life, although at the International Poetry Conference in Geneva, he sold W. H. Auden and Wallace Stevens each a Hoover.

Hassidic Tales, With a Guide to Their Interpretation by the Noted Scholar

Copyright © 1970 by Woody Allen. Reprinted from GETTING EVEN, by Woody Allen, by permission of Random House, Inc. Reprinted by permission; © 1970 The New Yorker Magazine, Inc.

A man journeyed to Chelm in order to seek the advice of Rabbi Ben Kaddish, the holiest of all ninth-century rabbis and perhaps the greatest *noodge* of the medieval era.

"Rabbi," the man asked, "where can I find peace?"

The Hassid surveyed him and said, "Quick, look behind you!"

The man turned around, and Rabbi Ben Kaddish smashed him in the back of the head with a candlestick. "Is that peaceful enough for you?" he chuckled, adjusting his *yarmulke*.

In this tale, a meaningless question is asked. Not only is the question meaningless but so is the man who journeys to Chelm to ask it. Not that he was so far away from Chelm to begin with, but why shouldn't he stay where he is? Why is he bothering Rabbi Ben Kaddish— the Rabbi doesn't have enough trouble? The truth is, the Rabbi's in over his head with gamblers, and he has also been named in a paternity case by a Mrs. Hecht. No, the point of this tale is that this man has nothing better to do with his time than journey around and get on people's nerves. For this, the Rabbi bashes his head in, which, according to the Torah, is one of the most subtle methods of showing concern. In a similar version of this tale, the Rabbi leaps on top of the man in a frenzy and carves the story of Ruth on his nose with a stylus.

Rabbi Raditz of Poland was a very short rabbi with a long beard, who was said to have inspired many pogroms with his sense of humor. One of his disciples asked, "Who did God like better—Moses or Abraham?"

"Abraham," the Zaddik said.

"But Moses led the Israelites to the Promised Land," said the disciple.

"All right, so Moses," the Zaddik answered.

"I understand, Rabbi. It was a stupid question."

"Not only that, but you're stupid, your wife's a *meeskeit*, and if you don't get off my foot you're excommunicated."

Here the Rabbi is asked to make a value judgment between Moses and Abraham. This is not an easy matter, particularly for a man who has never read the Bible and has been faking it. And what is meant by the hopelessly relative term "better"? What is "better" to the Rabbi is not necessarily "better" to his disciple. For instance, the Rabbi likes to sleep on his stomach. The disciple also likes to sleep on the Rabbi's stomach. The problem here is obvious. It should also be noted that to step on a rabbi's foot (as the disciple does in the tale) is a sin, according to the Torah, comparable to the fondling of matzos with any intent other than eating them.

A man who could not marry off his ugly daughter visited Rabbi Shimmel of Cracow. "My heart is heavy," he told the Rev, "because God has given me an ugly daughter."

"How ugly?" the Seer asked.

"If she were lying on a plate with a herring, you wouldn't be able to tell the difference."

The Seer of Cracow thought for a long time and finally asked, "What kind of herring?"

The man, taken aback by the query, thought quickly and said, "Er—Bismarck."

"Too bad," the Rabbi said. "If it was Maatjes, she'd have a better chance."

Here is a tale that illustrates the tragedy of transient qualities such as beauty. Does the girl actually resemble a herring? Why not? Have you seen some of the things walking around these days, particularly at resort areas? And even if she does, are not all creatures beautiful in God's eyes? Perhaps, but if a girl looks more at home in a jar of wine sauce than in an evening gown she's got big problems. Oddly enough, Rabbi Shimmel's own wife was said to resemble a squid, but this was only in the face, and she more than made up for it by her hacking cough—the point of which escapes me.

Rabbi Zwi Chaim Yisroel, an Orthodox scholar of the Torah and a man who developed whining to an art unheard of in the West, was unanimously hailed as the wisest man of the Renaissance by his fellow-Hebrews, who totalled a sixteenth of one per cent of the population. Once, while he was on his way to synagogue to celebrate the sacred Jewish holiday commemorating God's reneging on every promise, a woman stopped him and asked the following question: "Rabbi, why are we not allowed to eat pork?"

"We're *not*?" the Rev said incredulously. "Uh-oh."

This is one of the few stories in all Hassidic literature that deals with Hebrew law. The Rabbi knows he shouldn't eat pork; he doesn't care, though, because he *likes* pork. Not only does he like pork; he gets a kick out of rolling Easter eggs. In short, he cares very little about traditional Orthodoxy and regards God's covenant with Abraham as "just so much chin music." Why pork was proscribed by Hebraic law is still unclear, and some scholars believe that the Torah merely suggested not eating pork at certain restaurants.

Rabbi Baumel, the scholar of Vitebsk, decided to embark on a fast to protest the unfair law prohibiting Russian Jews from wearing loafers outside the ghetto. For sixteen weeks, the holy man lay on a crude pallet, staring at the ceiling and refusing nourishment of any kind. His pupils feared for his life, and then one day a woman came to his bedside and, leaning down to the learned scholar, asked, "Rabbi, what color hair did Esther have?" The Rev turned weakly on his side and faced her. "Look what she picks to ask me!" he said. "You know what kind of a headache I got from sixteen weeks without a bite!" With that, the Rabbi's disciples escorted her personally into the *sukkah*, where she ate bounteously from the horn of plenty until she got the tab.

This is a subtle treatment of the problem of pride and vanity, and seems to imply that fasting is a big mistake. Particularly on an empty stomach. Man does not bring on his own unhappiness, and suffering is really God's will, although why He gets such a kick out of it is beyond me. Certain Orthodox tribes believe suffering is the only way to redeem oneself, and scholars write of a cult called the Essenes, who deliberately went around bumping into walls. God, according to the later books of Moses, is benevolent, although there are still a great many subjects he'd rather not go into.

Rabbi Yekel of Zans, who had the best diction in the world until a Gentile stole his resonant underwear, dreamed three nights running that if he would only journey to Vorki he would find a great treasure there. Bidding his wife and children goodbye, he set out on a trip, saying he would return in ten days. Two years later, he was found wandering the Urals and emotionally involved with a panda. Cold and starving, the Rev was taken back to his home, where he was revived with steaming soup and flanken. Following that, he was given something to eat. After dinner, he told this story: Three days out of Zans, he was set upon by wild nomads. When they learned he was a Jew, they forced him to alter all their sports jackets and take in their trousers. As if this were not humiliation enough, they put sour cream in his ears and sealed them with wax. Finally, the Rabbi escaped and headed for the nearest town, winding up in the Urals instead, because he was ashamed to ask directions.

After telling the story, the Rabbi rose and went into his bedroom to sleep, and, behold, under his pillow was the treasure that he originally sought. Ecstatic, he got down and thanked God. Three days later, he was back wandering in the Urals again, this time in a rabbit suit.

The above small masterpiece amply illustrates the absurdity of mysticism. The Rabbi dreams *three* straight nights. The Five Books of Moses subtracted from the Ten Commandments leaves five. Minus the brothers Jacob and Esau leaves *three*. It was reasoning like this that led Rabbi Yitzhok Ben Levi, the great Jewish mystic, to hit the double at Aqueduct fifty-two days running and still wind up on relief.

ROGER ANGELL

Turtletaub and the Foul Distemper

From A DAY IN THE LIFE OF ROGER ANGELL, copyright ©
1970 by Roger Angell. Originally appeared in *The New Yorker*.
Reprinted by permission of Viking Penguin, Inc., and The
New Yorker Magazine, Inc.

The facts concerning last winter's mystifying New
England airplane accident—referred to variously in the
press as the "Vanishing Pilot Case" or the "Pancaked
Jetliner Puzzle"—are so fresh in the public mind that I
hesitate to reopen the matter, lest I be found guilty of
second-hand sensationalism. Yet the truth, or as much
of it as perhaps we will ever know, deserves to be set
forth, if only because it forms part of a far darker and
more tangled tale that certain authorities wish to sup-
press. Foremost among these is my old friend Inspector
Turtletaub of the Special Assignments Bureau, who first
told me the whole story and yet now claims concern for
my health and whimpers that "the world is not ready"
for the terrible truth. Lies, lies! My health has never
been better—ha, ha!—and here, sipping champagne

high above the Atlantic as I fly eastward to a new life, I pick up my pen and prepare to set down nothing less than a true history. I defy you, Lionel Turtletaub, to deny a syllable of it!

The details of the accident are easily set forth in précis. On a stormy March afternoon, a regularly scheduled airliner bound for Boston radioed the Logan tower to report a sudden failure of all navigational and directional instruments, as well as an undiagnosed and uncorrectable loss of power. The plane, in short, was lost and on the point of making a forced landing. This was the last radio contact. At 5:07 P.M. (E.S.T.), the inhabitants of Burbage Fens, Mass., a small village near Athol, heard the noise of a plane circling in low-lying clouds directly overhead—a roar that was abruptly silenced as the plane seemed to go into the ground in the environs of the Presumptionist Brothers monastery on a hillside just north of town. Hurrying there, the alarmed villagers were relieved to find the plane not only intact but entirely undamaged. The pilot, it could be seen, had made a brilliant wheels-up landing on the lawn of the monastery, formerly a large private estate. The monks, who had been at table in their refectory, were now trying to pry open the airliner's cabin doors. When they did so, they found the fifty-three passengers, the co-pilot, the engineer, and three stewardesses still strapped in their seats. None, it was quickly determined, had suffered so much as a bump or a scratch, yet all fifty-eight of them were semi-conscious. Moaning and shuddering, sometimes crying out in evident horror, they were quickly removed to a nearby hospital, where they were found to be suffering from shock. Recovery was rapid, and within twenty-four hours all of the survivors were released. To this day, however, not one of them has ventured a word of explanation as to the circumstances of the crash; if pressed by relatives or reporters, they grow pale, tremble uncontrollably, and make piteous attempts to leave the room. The findings of the National Transportation Safety Board have never been released. Nor has any information been given as to the whereabouts of the pilot, Captain Sebastian Moran, or of one of the monks, a novice known as Brother Larry, neither of whom has been seen since the moment of the crash.

There, as far as the public knows, the matter stands—just where it stood that evening six weeks ago when Inspector Turtletaub finished his press briefing and the last reporters, still muttering their complaints and questions, were led from his office. The last, that is, save I. Turtletaub looked up from his desk and saw me still in my accustomed chair.

"Didn't you hear me, Humberstone?" he growled. "That's all. There's the door."

"I heard you, Lionel," I said. I walked over to the door and snapped the lock. Then I threw my pencils and copy paper into the wastebasket. Then I held open my jacket for his inspection. "No visitors, no notes, no tapes," I said. "Now, Lionel, off the record..."

He rose and passed his hands nervously over his towering forehead. "I'd like to, Humberstone," he said unhappily. "But this, believe me, is a case like no other. It must remain forever veiled."

"Lionel," I said reproachfully. "This is me, Walt Humberstone—or rather, I. Have I ever violated a confidence?"

"You don't *understand!*" he burst out. "It's you I must protect, along with everybody else. Everyone out there!" He made a sweeping gesture with one hand. "They're not strong enough—*nobody* is strong enough to hear this!"

I smiled. "Remember the Shopworn Torso case?" I said. "Remember the Hoboken Glutton? I helped you with those, Lionel. I'm a tough old newshawk, so leave my feelings out of this. You've been on this case for weeks now, and I can see what it's doing to you. What was it—a new kind of hijack? Nerve gas, maybe? Weathermen? When will you make a collar?"

He shook his head again, threw himself into his chair, and then jumped up and resumed pacing. "No arrests, no arrests," he muttered to himself. "They're gone. Two twisted minds like that, once again loosed on the world... Who would believe it?"

"*I'd* believe it, Lionel," I said gently.

"Very well!" he cried, once more flinging himself behind his desk. "But remember—you begged me. Don't blame me later!" He took a bunch of keys from his side pocket, unlocked a drawer in his desk, and drew forth a bulging file.

"You said 'two twisted minds,'" I said. "Do you mean that the pilot and the monk were in it together?"

"Yes, of course," Turtletaub said, ruffling papers.

"But the monk was on the ground."

"Exactly. The co-pilot's evidence was perfectly clear about that. Seventeen passengers on the right-hand side of the plane confirmed his report. As the plane slithered across the lawn on its belly, the monk, later said to be 'Brother Larry,' ran forward from under a tree and seemed to be struck down by the right wing tip. They could all see him lying there as the plane stopped."

"But that sounds as it the monk was—" I began.

"Was *waiting* for the plane, yes," the Inspector said excitedly. "Was 'in it' with the pilot, yes. Was a joint planner and principal in a plot of truly diabolical premeditation! Was a criminal impostor of monstrous patience and cunning! Was, in short, a match for his partner in evil, the rascally Captain 'Sebastian Moran.' Ah, my friend, the arrogance of that name! The deranged brilliance of it!" He broke off and shook a sheaf of papers in my face. "They are the same pair!" he said fiercely. "The pattern is all too clear. Brother Larry is the North Woods Barrymore and Captain Moran is the Mad Editor. They have struck again!"

"What?" I cried, utterly dumbfounded now. "Who? When? Where?"

Inspector Turtletaub looked at me musingly. "Where shall we begin, Humberstone?" he said. "These are very deep waters."

He began, a few minutes later, with the Moses Paulding disappearance. I remembered the story—a minor mystery of a decade before. Moses Paulding, a respectable advertising account executive, had vanished after a cocktail party in Darien, where he lived. There had been a fracas of some kind. Paulding had walked out, never to be seen again.

"Moses Paulding," Turtletaub told me, "was suffering from Retardate Wildeanism, which means that he was never able to think of clever remarks until too late, usually the next morning. This is a commonplace ailment—we all have it to some degree—but Paulding's was a bad case. He was known in Darien as something of a dullard, yet at home in bed at night or while shaving the next morning he would suddenly burst out laughing as he thought of some flashing riposte, some edged apothegm, to throw into a conversation already hours or days dead. One day while driving in his car alone, he thought of a bon mot concerning Angela Thirkell, the English novelist, and was so convulsed that he had to pull over to the median strip to compose himself. That evening, he told his wife the joke—she filled me in on all this, much later—and explained to her that he had resolved to remember this one until it was needed. He planted it in his memory, so that he would be able to pluck it forth, casually and elegantly, at the very first mention of Angela Thirkell at somebody's dinner table or poolside party. The trouble was, of course, that Angela Thirkell wasn't exactly the best-known author in Darien. Oh, one may suppose that a few of his neighbors had heard of her or read her, but it wasn't a name that came up every day."

"Still isn't," I said, yawning.

"Very well," Turtletaub said, eying me. "*Bref*, nobody mentioned Angela Thirkell. There was our friend

Paulding preparing his one little firecracker before every dinner party and sociable—fondling and polishing it in his pocket, so to speak—and no one would light the fuse. Five years went by, and no Thirkell. She even died in that time, but no one in Darien noticed it or mentioned the fact in front of Paulding. The poor fellow was going mad. He'd almost forgotten, and then, on *der Tag*, he was a guest at a large summer lawn party when suddenly he thought he heard the magic sound of 'Angela Thirkell' drift through the evening air. The voice he'd heard was at the opposite end of a ninety-seven-foot veranda, but Paulding dropped his drink, left the people he was with, and ran over there, shoving through the other guests and upsetting a tray of sandwiches on the way. When he got there, it turned out to be a group of visitors who were total strangers to him—and the name they had dropped, by the way, was Studs Terkel, not Angela Thirkell—but Paulding pushed his way right in among them, and then, still panting but trying to appear offhand and debonair, he said, 'Well, *I've* always thought Angela Thirkell was a thquare.'"

"What!" I said, sitting up in my chair.

"That's what *they* said," said the Inspector. "They made him repeat it, the poor, doomed soul, and this time the whole party, easily sixty or seventy people, was listening, and nobody laughed. Nobody said a word, in fact. And at that instant, we may safely speculate, the mind of Moses Paulding cracked apart, like a dropped finger bowl. He walked slowly down the veranda steps and up the slate path to the driveway, and then turned and faced them. He lifted both his arms, and in a hair-raising, keening voice he cried, 'Revenge shall be miii-nnne!' He left, and no one has seen him—at least, under *that* name—to this day."

"Serves him right," I said, rubbing my burning temples. "But what about the plane? What about—"

Turtletaub held up his hand, consulted another

file, poured himself a sip of water from his decanter, and resumed. "Time: seven years ago," he said. "Place: a certain village in northernmost Quebec, well above Chicoutimi. The only inhabitants are trappers and lumberjacks, with the exception of the monks resident in a large local monastery. The only newspaper—"

"*Another* monastery?" I said.

"You've the makings of a detective, my good fellow," said the Inspector. "Yes. And the only newspaper is a modest bilingual weekly called *L'Éclaireur du Muskeg*. Properly modest, because there is normally no news whatsoever in this Godforsaken compound—no arrivals, no departures, few females, few diversions. The only excitement, in fact, is the annual stage presentation performed by the inhabitants of the monastery. This play is a regionally famous institution—or has been ever since its management was put entirely into the hands of a monk named—" He paused and consulted his notes. "Yes. Father Marcel Squegg."

"Funny name," I said.

"No," said Turtletaub grimly. "Not funny in the least. Well, Squegg, we have learned, was a first-class theatrical director and actor, an enthusiastic *metteur en scène* who succeeded in involving every one of his fellow-ecclesiastics in the annual mumming. There was a different presentation each autumn—one year a farce, the next a musical, the next Shakespeare, and so forth. Whatever its nature, Squegg directed, handled the casting and lighting, and played the leading role. He was brilliant, and his foremost supporter and press agent was the local newspaper, which, curiously enough, was also written and edited and printed entirely by one man, a friend of Squegg's."

"The Mad Editor!" I whispered. "And the North Woods Barrymore!"

"Exactly. Thus the editor dubbed him in the newspaper after Squegg's *succès fou* as Hamlet one year. He gave the monk the entire front page—photographs, headlines, and the better part of the rave notice. Unsurprisingly, such news quickly spread across the province, and soon word—the expected word—came up from the diocese, which permitted Squegg to put into motion the final details of the plan. He was summoned in by the abbot and reminded of the sin of pride. He was ordered to continue as director of forthcoming plays but was enjoined from further stardom. Squegg, of course, consented to abase himself. Well, the next year's item of repertory was a full-scale revival of 'Uncle Tom's Cabin,' and the customary sellout complement of woodsy first-nighters turned out to cheer their local Garrick—only to find his name absent from the bill. Squegg was in the play, in fact, but was not noticed, for he had cast himself as one of the dogs that follow Eliza across the ice in the melodramatic chase scene. He was completely encased in a bloodhound costume and was not recognized when he went sniffing and baying across the stage."

"I hope the play was better than this story," I said irritably. "This is the stupidest—"

"We'll see who's stupid!" Turtletaub snapped. "You are now in precisely the same position as those poor, helpless reubens. The Mad Editor and that fiendish priest have you at their mercy, and you don't even know it." He extracted a faded newspaper clipping from his file. "Here is the story about 'Uncle Tom's Cabin' that appeared in the *Éclaireur* the next morning. Never mind the review—just read the headline."

It was a banner right across the top of the page, and I read it out loud: "'PÈRE SQUEGG IN HOUND ROLE.'"

Turtletaub stooped and retrieved the clipping, which had fluttered from my fingers. I was at his desk, emptying the decanter over my head.

"The newspaper office was sacked that same morning," he went on. "The townspeople tore the place apart. By that time, of course, Paulding and the priest had long since departed, having made good their departure under cover of darkness. Paulding, we now know, was the editor. They were in it together, right from the start. We don't know where they met, of course, but we do know who Squegg was and how he got that way."

"No!" I spluttered. "*Please*, no. I don't want to hear about it. Nix."

Inexorably, he reached for another file and went on. "Originally, a Father Martin Quist, an unremarkable young priest in a poor Midwest parish," he intoned. "So poor, in fact, that they had to let out some of the rooms in the rectory to boarders, in order to make ends meet. Well, this was well back in the fifties, in the unlamented McCarthy era, and soon ugly stories were afloat to the effect that one of the boarders was a Communist and possibly an atheist. Parish morale declined and suspicions were rife, and one Sunday Father Quist determined to put an end to the matter. He arose in the pulpit after Mass—"

I put my hands up, as if to ward off a blow.

"—and told the congregation that there was nothing in it. The accused boarder, he said, was not a Catholic, but he certainly wasn't a Communist or an atheist. 'In fact,' he told them, holding back a smile, 'I can assure you that we have nothing here but an unconfirmed roomer.'" Turtletaub flicked me a glance. "Maybe I should spell that out for you," he said. "He meant—"

"I *know* what he meant!" I said, gagging. "A man like that— Why, I would have— Excommunication!"

"Not quite," said the Inspector, "but he was out of office and out of the parish by nightfall. Exile and Squeggdom ensued. Before he left town, you see, he, too, made a public vow of revenge. Exactly like Paulding."

"Which brings your story full circle," I said, rising hastily and grabbing for my raincoat. "And a terrible story it's been, too. Well, thanks, Lionel, and—"

"Sit down!" Turtletaub thundered. "We haven't even come to the plane crash yet. And you asked for this—remember?"

The next hour dragged by painfully as the Inspector described his own involvement in the case—the urgent request for his services, first from the Canadian Mounties, then by Interpol; the months of careful backtracking and painstaking police work that uncovered the identities of the two lunatics; and the fears, kept very secret, of forensic medical experts that the Paulding-Quist syndrome might prove in some way to be contagious, thus threatening the Western mind with a truly terrifying new madness. These fears, in fact, were deepened by the number of parallel cases that distracted Turtletaub from his manhunt. There were indeed other victims of the foul distemper, and Turtletaub, in his methodical manner, spared me none of the details.

"Now, you take the Lord Tweedy business, back in '65," he said. "That certainly *sounded* like Paulding's work. A shocking tale. A wealthy British tourist had arrived in a little Alpine village one afternoon, where he joined a crowd of local citizens watching a burning chalet. Could he have *lit* that fire? Possibly. We shall never know. As the flames died down, he observed quietly that it was rather early in the season to see Swiss charred. The man hadn't counted on the multilingual capacities of the natives, for by the time I arrived in the Bernese Oberland, two days later, all traces of his corpse had been eradicated. We suspect that he lies at the foot of the Reichenbach Fall. Only a study of his signature in the register at the local inn convinced me that he could not have been Paulding. Can you hear me down there?"

I was lying under his desk, with my head partially concealed in his overturned wastebasket, and I waved one hand feebly to indicate continuing consciousness.

"Similarly," Turtletaub resumed, "the tragic affair of the Black Retainer *could* have been Quist-Squegg's work—or so I believed when I first investigated. The difficulty of playing a Negro butler with sufficient servile aplomb as to take in the entire Culpepper family, as well as all the other plantation hands, is a challenge that would attract a great actor. Surely you remember the case—it led to the overnight revival of sixteen Klan chapters in South Carolina alone. My investigations on the scene, however, proved the unlikelihood of premeditation, and I had to absolve our two loonies of any involvement. To be sure, the aged retainer knew that his master, Colonel Gaylord Culpepper, was a hopeless alcoholic who regularly did away with fourteen mint juleps before lunchtime, but how could he have anticipated that on that particular day the Colonel, in stumbling search of another bottle of bourbon, would pass out in the pantry, crashing headlong in a welter of comestibles? And how could he have arranged matters so that, in his fall, the Colonel would pull down upon himself a two-pound, economy-size box of Hershey's Instant Cocoa? No, it was pure accident, and the missing butler—who has so far escaped apprehension—was but a chance victim suddenly struck down by this sinister new affliction. His mistress, you see, noting the absence of the family rumhound from the environs of the decanter, rang the bell, and when the courtly servitor had shuffled into the room she said, 'Cudjo, wheah's the Colonel?' How the poor fellow must have trembled as he saw the pit suddenly yawn at his feet! He could not help himself. He bowed and murmured, 'Massa's in de cocoa grounds.'"

I sprang up from under Turtletaub's desk, conking my head on the typewriter table, and flew to the window. "Air!" I gasped, clawing at the latch. "Give me air!"

"Yes, the airplane," Turtletaub continued, closing his eyes and forming a steeple with his fingers. "It's time to sum up. For all my efforts, Paulding-Moran and his evil partner remained undetected right up to the moment last month when their paths, by mad pre-arrangement, converged. Picture the drama. Paulding, in the pilot's seat, makes certain secret adjustments to the controls to destroy all navigational signals and diminish power. He alerts the passengers to their plight, and the 'lost' plane plummets toward its rendezvous on the hilltop. As the jet slithers across the grass, 'Brother Larry' bursts from hiding, dashes forward, and *pretends* to be struck down by the wing tip. The plane stops, the pilot coolly makes his report to the strapped-down passengers and crew, and, a moment later, he and his accomplice make good their escape, leaving half a hundred helpless victims in a condition of mass psycholepsy. *Finis*.''

"'*Finis*'?" I croaked. "But—but what *happened*?"

Turtletaub looked at me for an instant, puzzled. "Oh," he said at last, "didn't I tell you before? After the plane stopped moving, Paulding turned on the intercom and announced, "Well, folks, out of the flying plan and into the friar.' But, my dear fellow—" And with a troubled face he sprang toward me as I toppled forward gratefully into oblivion.

My champagne glass is empty; the plane dips toward Paris. My tale is nearly done. No need to recount the long, painful weeks of my illness, the battle for the cloudy fortress of my mind. Suffice it to say that while cleverly feigning coma one morning I overheard the rascally Turtletaub—that devoted "friend!," that defender of public weal!—plotting with a band of white-garbed quacks for my permanent sequestration! "I blame myself," the villain told them again and again. "I should have seen it coming."

What he should have seen coming was my escape, that very evening. What he could *never* have seen coming was my present guise, the nature of my forthcoming career, and—*hee, hee, hee!*—my name. Shall I offer you a peep at my passport? Very well—there! You start back in surprise. It cannot be, you think! Ah, but it is. Pray let me introduce myself—"Lionel Turtletaub," at your disposal.

Lionel Turtletaub, who, by means of certain cleverly dispatched and intercepted cables, will shortly begin tenure as a detective on loan to the Sûreté. There, with full access to criminal files, I shall find my first accomplice. A Chinese, a Malay perhaps—it doesn't matter; he need only be Oriental. Then, within weeks, I select my victim. Already I can see her—a pert Parisian widow, habituated to a certain elegance, perhaps a young vicomtesse. *Pauvre chérie*, she is soon to be troubled by a series of minor robberies. First a ring, then a brooch, then the lavaliere once presented to her by the late vicomte himself. The police are called; a master detective, an American Maigret, comes forward to offer his services. Turtletaub to the rescue! There is another robbery, though, and then another. Madame is disconsolate, but M. L'Inspecteur vows to crack the case. He spends hours at her flat, examining fingerprints. A friendliness, a genuine warmth, seems to deepen between them. He offers certain gallantries; blushing, she dismisses them.

Then, on a warm night, Madame hears a sound, sees a shadow. She sits up in bed and screams! Through the French window springs Turtletaub, *pistolet* in hand. The trap has been sprung. His flashlight darts here, there, then focusses on the closet. A scuffle, an oath, and then out from behind Madame's dresses comes the criminal, hands high in the air. Still keeping him covered, Turtletaub snaps on the bedroom lights. The robber is wearing silk slippers, a long queue, and an angry mandarin scowl. M. L'Inspecteur smiles at his distraught client, who charmingly pulls the coverlet higher toward her chin. Bowing, Turtletaub murmurs, "At last, Madame, I have discovered the Chink in your armoire!"

The no-smoking light is on: Paris. Paulding, *cher maître!* Quist, *mon semblable!* Ye shall be revenged!

MICHAEL ARLEN

More, and Still More, Memories of the Nineteen-Twenties

Reprinted by permission; © 1960 The New Yorker Magazine, Inc.

What a summer! Everyone was in the South of France. Willie Maugham was at Antibes. Margot Asquith was at Jimmy Sheean's. Jimmy Sheean was at Margot Asquith's. In June, we all went up to Paris to watch the Prince of Wales, then the most popular man of his time, fall off his horse at Auteuil. When he did, the crowd rushed across the track, picked up the young heir apparent, and carried him on their shoulders all the way to his room at the Ritz. Despite the twenty-two-mile walk through heavy traffic, with the Prince in obvious pain from a broken collarbone, it was a stirring occasion.

Later, in the lobby of the hotel, I noticed a slight, dark-haired American lady making her way discreetly toward the service elevator. "We shall be hearing more about that girl," I remember remarking to Sherwood Anderson, who was covering the spectacle for the Seattle *Post-Intelligencer*. I was right. That girl was Helen Wills Moody.

This was in 1928. Back in New York, Jimmy Walker was mayor and the whole city had embarked on a frenzy of high spirits and wild living. On Broadway, Fred and Adele Astaire, fresh from a season's triumphs in "Kumquats of 1928," were polishing new routines for the opening of "Kumquats of 1929." Out in Hollywood, a young Spanish actor, Rodolpho d'Antonguolla, was already making a name for himself (Rudolph Valentino), subject to approval by the Los Angeles District Court. It was the era of prohibition, bootleg gin, and the infield single. Charles D. Flent was the best-loved man in America, and Calvin Coolidge was in the White House.

We were living at the time in a fashionable apartment on upper Fifth Avenue. On the advice of Bascomb W. Bascomb, my father had invested heavily in the rising bail-bond market, and our house was then a gathering place for many of the famous luminaries of the day. On the same evening, one might see such glittering personages as William S. (Big Bill) Thompson, William T. (Big Bill) Tilden, or William S. (Big Bill) Hart. Often, Otto Kahn, the banker, would come bustling in late in the evening with a bagful of money or Radio stock, which he would distribute to the guests. Noël Coward frequently made an appearance, as well as many other literary figures of the time: Bunny Wilson, Victor Hugo, Joseph Moncure March, Bruno Brockton. Sad, clever Bruno Brockton. If only he had published!

One of the best-known gatherings in New York in this period was the famous Oxford Group, a collection of writers, playwrights, and wits who met every Wednesday evening for lunch in the old Oxford Hotel, on Thirty-seventh Street. The members of the Oxford Group had a reputation for dazzling humor and repartee, to say nothing of sheer animal hunger, and to be invited to their table was one of the most sought-after honors that could befall a visitor to the city. It was at one of these lunches, I recall, that the famous exchange between S. S. VanFlogel, the columnist, and Leo Tolstoy, the Russian novelist and count, took place. Tolstoy, whose novel "War and Peace" had earlier attracted much critical attention, had been travelling incognito in New York on the I.R.T., and was brought to the lunch late one evening by John Cameron Gilpin, the artist. Swiftly, the conversation turned to a discussion of the celebrated novel. It was widely known in New York that VanFlogel had had it "in" for Tolstoy for some time, and, suddenly, in a caustic tone, he asked the Russian if he wouldn't have written the book differently if he "had been a woman." There was a stunned silence. VanFlogel's biting wit was feared as far north as Sixty-third Street, and it was doubtful whether the elderly Russian could hold his own against the columnist. Tolstoy looked around him at the company. His eyes met Gilpin's. "Which woman?" he replied quickly. The rest is history.

This was the year when the stock market began its unparalleled rise. Men were making fortunes overnight. A few even made money during the day. A veritable fever, or fervor, of speculation swept Wall Street, which now, thanks to the Securities and Exchange Commission, higher margin rates, sound money, cold feet, and the Kellogg-Briand Pact, is no longer possible. It was the Golden Age of Sport. Dempsey knocked out Carpentier. Tunney knocked out Dempsey. Babe Ruth hit five hundred and three home runs. Charles D. Flent was the most popular man in America, and Francis X. Bushman was in the White House, visiting Calvin Coolidge.

Scott Fitzgerald was much in the news at this time, and his exploits were helping to set the pace for his generation. Fitzgerald, who had attended Princeton some years earlier, had been dropped from the football squad for being "too thin," and had always regretted not having had a chance to play John O'Hara's Yale team in the Bowl. One evening, toward the end of the football season, we were all sitting around in the Plaza fountain—Maxwell Perkins, Burton Rascoe, K. K. Huneker, Ellsworth Vines, Fitzgerald, and myself—when Fitzgerald leaped to his feet and cried, "Let's go up to New Haven and beard the bulldog!" Rascoe quickly commandeered a carriage from the hack stand on Fifty-ninth Street, and we all piled in for the trip to Connecticut. By the time we reached New Haven, the Yale team had already left the practice field, but Fitzgerald jumped out of the carriage and ran through the college quadrangles yelling, "Fire in the engine room, men! Everybody out to the Bowl!" What a night that was! The undergraduates poured out of the dormitories and we all swept out to the great stadium. By this time, Fitzgerald and the rest of us had dressed in football gear, but Yale unfortunately fielded its first lacrosse team. I remember Fitzgerald turning to me as we all trooped back to the dressing room and saying, "Twenty years from now, we shall all have a good laugh over this." Sad, brilliant Scott Fitzgerald. Was he more than just a regional writer? I have always maintained that he was.

My most lasting memory of the times, however, is of the day I went, with John Middleton Mommsen, to meet the Long Eagle, the young aviator whose daring exploits and pioneering spirit had made him the most famous figure in the land. We found the youthful pilot working in overalls beside a frail little craft, apparently made out of buckboard and canvas, with the legend "Spirit of St. Louis" hand-stencilled on its side. He spun the propeller. The engine gave a few fitful coughs and lay still. He spun it again. There was no response. The third time, he put his whole lanky body into the effort. The engine roared into action. Lindbergh—for it was he—stepped back and turned toward us. "It's a serviceable machine," he said shyly, "but it will never replace the Zeppelin."

How little the three of us knew then. War clouds were already gathering over Europe. The Zeppelin was doomed.

DONALD BARTHELME

Bunny Image, Loss of: The Case of Bitsy S.

Reprinted with the permission of Farrar, Straus & Giroux, Inc. from GUILTY PLEASURES by Donald Barthelme, copyright © 1963, 1964, 1965, 1966, 1968, 1969, 1970, 1971, 1972, 1973, 1974 by Donald Barthelme.

Four Playboy bunnies, discharged two weeks ago for having lost their "bunny image," appeared before the State Commission on Human Rights yesterday to press their complaint that Playboy practices sexual and age discrimination...

...Miss [Patti] Columbo said Tony LeMay, the "international bunny mother," told her: "You have changed from a girl to a woman. You look old. You have lost your bunny image."

"We have none of the characteristics which are considered loss of bunny image," said Nancy Phillips,

one of the four. "Crinkling eyelids, sagging breasts, stretch marks, crepey necks, and drooping derrières," she said, are cited in Playboy literature as defects that will ruin the career of a bunny.

> *Mario Staub, general manager of the club since 1971, asserted: "Termination for bunny image has always been company practice... They have simply lost their bunny image—that attractive, fresh, youthful look they had when they started."*

—*The New York Times*

INTRODUCTION

Loss of bunny image, or Staub's syndrome, was first identified as a distinct clinical entity by Altmann. Bunny image, or the plastic representation of one's corporeal self as differentiated in specific ways from the corporeal selves of others, was discussed by Steinem and others as early as 1963. But it was Altmann who refined the concept and, more particularly, the cluster of pathologies associated with its loss. It is true that Altmann's work is indebted to that of Pick, whose valuable discussion of the phenomenon of the "phantom limb" following amputation provided, as Altmann has acknowledged, a fruitful hint. But it was the case of Bitsy S., the protocol of which follows, that gave this investigator his most important insights, and his place in the literature of body disturbances.

CASE REPORT

Bitsy S., an attractive white female of twenty-eight, was admitted to Bellevue Hospital complaining that she could not find, physically locate, her own body. It was "gone," she said, and added that she needed it and wanted it back. She further said that she had looked everywhere for it, that it was absolutely nowhere to be found, and that she had thought of going to the police about the matter but had decided instead to resort to the hospital because she felt that the police might think she was "strange." The case was first diagnosed as one of simple amnesia, but when the patient did not respond to routine procedures (including hypnosis), Altmann was consulted.

Altmann began with a series of questions.

(Investigator grasps left hand of patient, bringing it to patient's eye level.)

"What is this?"

"A hand."

"Right or left?"

(Patient examines hand carefully.)

"Left."

"Whose hand is it?"

"I don't know."

"To what is the hand attached?"

(Patient studies hand and forearm.)

"Arm."

"Whose arm?"

"I don't know."

"Is it your arm?"

"No. I don't have an arm."

(Investigator gently moves his hand up the arm in a series of light touches, finally coming to rest on the patient's left shoulder.)

"What is this?"

"Shoulder."

"Your shoulder?"

"No. I don't have a shoulder."

"*Somebody's* shoulder."

(The patient considers this for a moment.)

"Probably. Maybe."

(The investigator squeezes the shoulder slightly— a friendly squeeze.)

The subject then said, in a singsong voice:

"Please, sir, you are not allowed to touch the Bunnies."

This was, of course, Altmann's first clue. In connection with his studies of horror vacui he had quite naturally gravitated toward the New York Playboy Club and had, in fact, been a keyholder since its inception.

DONALD BARTHELME

Thus the statement "Please, sir, you are not allowed to touch the Bunnies" was not an unfamiliar one. He immediately asked:

"Are you a Bunny?"

"No," she said. "I am not a Bunny."

"If you are not a Bunny then why are you a member of the class of persons that I am not allowed to touch?"

There was no response from the patient.

"Were you ever a Bunny?"

"Yesterday."

"You were a Bunny yesterday?"

"Yesterday I was a Bunny and today I am not a Bunny. I was terminated. For loss of bunny image."

"What is 'bunny image'?"

"The attractive, fresh, youthful look I had when I started. The International Bunny Mother came to me and said: 'You have changed from a girl into a woman. You look old. You have lost your bunny image.' Then she cut off my bunny tail, with a pair of tin snips. Then she asked for my ears back. I gave her my ears back. I was weeping. I asked her why. That was a mistake. She told me. Crinkling eyelids. Crepey neck. Drooping derrière. I mentioned that I had been pinched thrice on that derrière the night before. She said that that was not enough, that I was below the national average for pinches-per-night. I said that I slept every night in a bathtub filled to the brim with Skin Life, by Helena Rubinstein. She said that she appreciated my 'desire' but that it was time to cut the squad and the rookies coming up from the farm clubs were growing impatient. I said I would stuff extra Kleenex into the top of my bunny costume, if that would help. She said that some people just didn't know when it was time to hang it up. Loss of bunny image, she said, was more than a physical thing. There were intangibles involved. I asked for an example of an intangible. She looked out of the window and said she had to catch a plane for Chicago. And then this morning I woke up and couldn't find my body. It was gone. Naturally I looked in the mirror first but there was nothing in the mirror—just mirror. Then I tried to touch my toes but when I tried to touch my toes there were no toes and no fingers to touch them with. Then I began to get worried."

(The investigator then complimented the patient warmly on her physical appearance, which was in fact, as noted above, quite feminine, attractive, and pleasing.)

"Who are you talking about?" she asked.

"You."

"You is lost," she said. "Somewhere all the lost bunny images are, each Bunny calling for its Bunny Mother, each lost bunny image still somewhere stuffing plastic laundry bags into the bosom of its bunny costume, bunny tails still pert, white, oh so white, each lost bunny image still practicing the Bunny Stance, the Bunny Dip—"

The investigator then began a course of Teddy Bear therapy, in which the subject is gradually introduced to an object which is not the subject but which holds in common with the subject certain physical features (arms, legs, head, etc.) which, in time, enable the patient to "find" himself—in this instance, herself—by equating the specific appurtenances of the teddy bear with his or her own body parts. Although this course of treatment shamelessly trades upon the natural love of human beings for teddy bears, it was felt that it was not in essence more manipulative than other therapies. A more dangerous contraindication was, of course, the unfortunate parity between "bunny" and "teddy bear"—the problems involved being obvious. Altmann nevertheless decided that it was the therapy of choice and its use was validated by the fact that Bitsy S. has once again "found" her own body and, indeed, has been able to construct a mature, stable, and "giving" relationship with a member of the medical profession.

CONCLUSION
The life of man, as Vince Lombardi said, is nasty, brutish, and short.

HENRY BEARD

Kiss Off,
Cruel World

Copyright © 1970. National Lampoon, Inc. Reprinted with permission.

People have always put a lot of stock in first impressions, but actually, last impressions are pretty important, too. No one remembers what Caesar said to the Helvetians, but who does not know the line, "*Et tu, Brute*"? Obviously, if Caesar had muttered those words while passing Brutus in the Serpentarium or whatever it was, they wouldn't have had much weight; and if, after being stabbed, he had said, "*In hoc signo vinces*" (from many, one) or "*Fero ferre tuli latus*" (you've ruined my toga), history would not have been so kind. All of this goes to show that your last words shouldn't be wasted. (As a matter of fact, unless you plan to be the first man on Mars or to make some important discovery, like who the Helvetians were, they're the only words of yours anyone is going to pay any attention to. Your only other opportunity for spoken importance you've already thrown away, unless of course you have yet to speak your first words. And even if your mother has an electroplated record of your first deathless burbles hidden away with your quoits trophies and the Empire State Building thermometer, it's dollars to diapers you weren't too heavily committed to any of the Indo-European tongues at the time, and the kind of people who are likely to quote you spend a lot of their time talking to trees and doing imitations of rocks.)

Unfortunately, to be quite frank, the odds of your actually voicing something memorable in the way of last words are pretty slim. Not only are the impressive-looking hospital machines in which the majority of our citizens get whisked across the Styx not too conducive to idle chatter, but the likelihood of your saying something final and golden like "Lay me under the greenwood tree" or "Give me some torpedoes to damn" and lingering for another 20 years is just as strong as the possibility of your passing to the nether shore with something fine unspoken.

On the other hand, if you're planning an early exit, it's another story entirely, and here there's room for some sobering statistics (and anyone who knows the population of Kansas or how many times around the world the cables of the George Washington Bridge will stretch knows just how sobering statistics can be). In Scandinavia, which leads the world in suicides (the Benelux countries are second, with the Netherlands, Belgium and Luxembourg tied for a close third), 56 percent of the suicides left no notes, 22 percent left illegible notes, 11 percent left notes considered "obvious"

(Stockholm Star) or "maudlin" *(Swedish Meatball)*. Only 7 percent of the notes had subtitles, and all but 2 percent contained at least one of the following phrases: "As I cross the bar," "It's a far better thing," and "Death before dishonor." All of this is especially sobering since the vast majority of these unfortunates missed a golden opportunity. The power of *"Et tu, Brute,"* after all, is that it drove Brutus nuts and eventually to suicide, and the only true measure of the success of a suicide note is in how many more suicides can be directly attributed to it. Frankly, if you're no poet, forget the history books, drop the dactyls and concentrate on impact. At the very least, your note should cause in two or three key readers one of the following reactions:

A. Frustrated Anger ("I could kill him.")
B. Remorse/Regret ("I could kill myself.")
C. Bananas ("I could kill everyone on my block.")

The following brief case histories are presented for inspiration rather than imitation, but they show how the average man with a self-destructive bent can make his last words count....

Arthur K. was a successful banker in a major Midwestern city, a man with no apparent worries or fears. In a bizarre accident, he fell out the window of his 12th-story office while watching a parade but escaped all save the most minor injuries when he crashed through seven successive layers of bunting and landed in a float representing the startling triumphs of Natural Down Chicken Feathers (a major product of the region) over Cheap Substitutes and Imported Stuffing Matter. Unfortunately, however, on his way down, his life passed before his eyes, as often happens, and what he saw so depressed him that he resolved to do himself in. Chief among the sources of his depression were his wife, Madge K. (the former Madge M.), and their children, Arthur Jr., Sally, and the Thing. He also realized that the family dog,

Sheddy, probably commanded more affection, pound for pound, than he did, and this particularly depressed him, since he had lovingly fed the beast by hand from his own medicine chest on several occasions. Arthur's exit was nicely handled, and his suicide note was a minor masterpiece. It was neatly handwritten on the crumpled torn half of a piece of notepaper which had clearly spent some time "in the mandible region of a canine interloper," as the inspecting officer observed at the inquest. Oddly, a careful dissection of Sheddy produced nothing. What was left of the note read:

...paces past the rotisserie and dig. It's in tens and twenties and there was $800,000 the last time I looked. I really feel silly telling you this, but I never did put much trust in banks. I know this must be a shock to you and the kids, but I know you'll make out just fine. Please see that Grandma gets the Ming vase.

Needless to say, the extensive excavation, first subtly with beach tools, then later with Caterpillar bulldozers, yielded nothing beyond Sheddy's impressive collection of soup bones and the broken shards of a Ming vase, though it did somewhat lower the value of the property. Mrs. K. went quite crazy and slew nine with a lawn flamingo before they could stop her. The kids were sold to a cereal company.

In every field of endeavor, there is at least one da Vinci, and in the rather rarefied realm of suicide notes, it is, or rather, was, Roger F. An actor and amateur movie-maker of no talent, Roger had bridled for several years under what he felt was the unfair and prejudiced criticism of the reviewers of every newspaper in his city. He was found by a friend, an unsuccessful free-lance photographer, hanging from an electric cord in a room full of gas. Pinned to his shirt was a piece of paper. The picture of this classic tableau ran in half the city's papers, the story of the suicide in all of them. Two papers carried articles linking the suicide with drugs. It was thus quite baffling when the police released the contents of the note:

1 pair of socks
2 shirts
3 towels
1 handkerchief
4 sets underwear
No Starch

It was only a matter of time before the police came upon a small movie camera by a laundry bag in the corner of the room, and, hoping on a long chance that its contents might yield some clue to the happenings, developed the film. The result, a little out of focus but otherwise professional, was Roger's masterpiece, and his real suicide note. The film began jumpily, as if the camera had been accidentally bumped, and Roger was seen filling a bag of laundry and preparing a list, which kept slipping behind a bureau or onto the floor or into the bag. It then showed Roger as he pinned the list to his shirt, put the bag in the corner, then stopped and sniffed the air curiously. He looked at the ceiling, where a gas meter was bolted, and from which hung a series of electrical wires. Then, in the best performance of his career, he moved a very rickety stepladder to the center of the room and, his face clearly showing his fear of heights, climbed the ladder, pretended to slip, and hanged himself.

In less than a week, Roger's wife stepped forward and, with the proceeds of the sale of Roger's cameras, sued all 11 newspapers for libel and slander. The suit took four and a half years, but she eventually collected $1,745,000 and court costs. The film of Roger's suicide became an underground classic and grossed $300,000.

The newspapers were more circumspect in reporting the suicides, within a period of two months, of one of the reviewers, four reporters and one editor.

A small example of the art, but worth reporting, was the exit of Sam G. (also known as Sammy G. and Sam the G.), a middle-level gangster. Hounded by the Internal Revenue Service, his wife, the Justice Department and the Mob, he decided to take the easy way out. He was found in his plush suburban home in a room littered with suicide notes. There were 17 in all, and they were identical:

I, Samuel G., did this myself. My good friends Babbo S. and Gino V. had nothing to do with this. They are innocent and know nothing about it. They certainly are clean. I swear it.

The typewriter, of course, matched none in Sam's house; he had misspelled his name on all the notes; and on a dictaphone, which lay on the floor, he had left for his wife a taped message full of gasps and pauses:

"Suzy, Swiss Bank Account, Union Zurich Bank, 121 Rue des Cloches Cucues, Zurich 12, Switzerland, Canton Zurich, the number is... is..."

The last example is more typical of the standard approach. Albert P. was a reasonably successful accountant, married, with no children. His reasons for doing himself in were obscure, but friends cite a nagging wife and an unpleasant mother-in-law. He dropped a number of what psychiatrists call "death hints" in the days before his final action. "I'm going to kill myself," he reportedly told his wife, "so don't invite anyone over for a while." He also gave away some suits to the Salvation Army, canceled his subscriptions and cut down the milk delivery. He was found in the swimming pool festooned with leis made from strung-together vacuum attachments and covered with peanut butter. His note, sealed in a plastic bag, read:

LAST WILL AND TESTAMENT OF ALBERT P.
Being of sound mind and body, I, Albert P., attest that this is my only true will and direct that apportionments of my estate be made from it. According to a vision, in which the great god Vishnu came to me in the guise of a hand laundry and bade me seek the Kubafooba, the path to greater wisdom through immersion in sandwich spreads, I have decided to leave my entire estate to my beloved mother-in-law, Martha F., whose cosmic oneness is a source of comfort to me.

The will was in probate for 22 years.

BURTON BERNSTEIN

B.B. Turns
Into René

Reprinted by permission; © 1962 The New Yorker Magazine, Inc.

The following, I'm afraid, is an apology to my generally understanding, if taxed, relatives, friends, and acquaintances, who have put up with a good deal of peculiar behavior on my part recently. I can only hope that this, in some small way, will explain what I've been through, and that those affected will feel free to call me up and invite me into their homes again sometime.

It began on a drizzly Wednesday morning. I had extracted my mail from the box in the vestibule of my apartment house and trotted off, under the protection of my umbrella, to catch a downtown bus to my office.

Once settled in a seat, I placed the handful of dull-looking envelopes in my lap and prepared to open the top one. But something kept me from immediately performing this simple, habitual task. It was my name. It called to me mysteriously from the center of the envelope in typed capital letters: "BURTON BERNSTEIN." Not much of a name—one perhaps distinguished only by its alliteration and quantity of vowels—and there was certainly nothing novel about it to *me*. However, for some reason that gray morning, its arrangement of letters seemed to mesmerize me. "BURTON BERNSTEIN." I continued to stare at it and suddenly, inexplicably, I found myself anagramming it. The "S," the "I," and an "R" leaped out at me in that order, and the rest was easy. Before the bus had travelled two more blocks, I had created a whole new name—Sir Bennett Broun.

"Not at all bad," I muttered happily, causing the matron next to me to answer, "What?"

"I merely remarked," I went on uncontrollably, "that it wasn't at all bad." With deft manipulations, I rolled my brolly tight and rose to leave the omnibus. "And now, if you'll excuse me, I really must be going. Good morning."

The circular motions the matron was making with her right index finger near her temple did not shock me back to reality, and neither did the fact that I had left the bus twenty blocks short of my destination. With a gait barely distinguishable from that of a brigadier serving his twelfth consecutive year with the Khyber Rifles, I went on my way, unmindful of the drizzle. But somewhere in one of the ensuing rain-darkened blocks, it happened again. The name René Bons-Bruttin skittered into focus before my mind's eye. My smartly furled umbrella instantly became a Maurice Chevalier walking stick, and I was amazed to discover that I had winked charmingly, and rather successfully, at several female pedestrians.

"Morning, sir," said the elevator starter at my office building. "Nasty weather out, isn't it? But I don't think it'll last till noon."

"*Plus ça change, plus c'est la même chose,*" I responded, with a jaunty toss of my head. "*Bonjour, mon vieux.*" I jigged nimbly into the elevator, not inhibiting a few whistled bars of "Mimi."

I know now that I never should have gone into that elevator. Reason should have turned me on my heels and sent me straight home to bed, where I could have worked out the whole problem in the privacy of my home. But, no. Willingly, excitedly, I plunged ahead.

"Good morning," said the receptionist.

"Hi, chick," I cackled. "Look here, baby, as far as you're concerned, ol' No. 1, yours truly, Buster Binnerton, America's most desirable rich playboy, is out to everyone today. Everyone, that is, except Ernest ('Bub') Rinton, the Texas oil tycoon, and Norbreet Ibn Tuns, his Cadillac-driving business partner and the Scourge of the Persian Gulf. By the way, honey, what's on for tonight? Le Club Elmo, or how about a chopper ride out to my place in the Hamptons?"

The receptionist fled to the ladies' room and I continued to my office. No sooner had I settled myself at my desk than the phone rang. Could this be the tipoff? Had they found me out? Was my true identity—that of Tornbein Stubner, the notorious fugitive *Obersturmbannführer*—finally revealed to Robert St. Bunnien, the hard-living, wily British MI5 detective-adventurer who had been on my trail ever since '46?

I allowed my monocle to fall and wisely assumed one of my aliases. "*Pronto,*" I drawled into the mouthpiece. "Strebenni speaking. Bruno T. Strebenni, the olive-oil king. *Ciao.*"

"*Who*? Who is this?" said an alarmed feminine voice.

"Oh, it is you, my dear," I said to my wife, retaining only a trace of my refined Milanese accent.

"What's the matter with you?" she asked. "Have you gone crazy?"

I dared not answer.

"Well, you can explain later. Anyway, the Berinsons phoned and want to know if we can come over to their place tonight for dinner."

"Not *Burnett* Berinson, the noted and respected art critic?" I chirped, after some rapid anagrammatic doodling.

"I don't know," my wife said hopelessly. "*I'm* talking about George and Shirley Berinson, of course. Our dear friends, remember? They're having a few people over and—"

"We can't," I interrupted. "Just this morning, I ran into my old pal from the Cree reservation—Toni N. Ten Rubbers. You've certainly heard me speak of him. Well, I've invited him for dinner tonight. Just make something simple—potlatch or pemmican or bison shank. He's not fussy and he's a terrific guy, except when he drinks. You'll love him."

There was a click, and I was left mumbling to myself. That was no way to treat Torst Inrubbenen, the Olympic record-holding Finnish distance runner.

The rest of the day went like that.

I arrived home that night sunken-eyed and exhausted. The maid was just finishing up her cleaning and I wearily got out my checkbook to pay her. "Let's see," I said, figuring fast. "That would be ten dollars, payable to Rubistone Brennt, right?"

"But my name is Eloise," she said, surveying me

out of the corner of her left eye. "You know, Eloise? Eloise Armstrong?"

I placated her with a ten-dollar bill, and she bolted from the room.

My wife wouldn't speak to me, except to announce that she was going over to the Berinsons for drinks and dinner and that I could fend for myself. She prescribed some hot milk, two aspirins, and a lot of sleep. Then she, too, left.

I mixed myself a vodka Martini and turned on the television set. Huntley and Brinkley were exchanging some significant smirks as a prelude to a film clip of an important Senate committee hearing. I lay down on the couch to watch.

The stern-visaged, inscrutable Sen. Trentin Burbo was presiding. "Do yo' honestly believe, suh, that we senators should confirm yo' appointment as Sec'tary of State when yo' admittedly allow as to how you suffer from chronic polyanagramophrenia?" he asked me coldly.

"Sounds like a natural security risk to me," piped up the diminutive Sen. Robin Tut (R., Neb.).

"Let's hear him out, give him a chance," said Sen. T. T. Nubbin (R., Ore.), a robust, white-maned gentleman I immediately felt was a friend.

Fortunately, I had engaged the greatest trial lawyer in the country as my counsel—none other than the much publicized, odds-battling New York attorney Benson Ruttenrib. "Gentlemen," he began, commanding the complete attention of those present with his piercing eyes and booming voice. "May I humbly request that before my distinguished client testifies, I be permitted to read from a laudatory statement on his behalf signed by some of the greatest names in statesmanship, politics, science, and industry?"

"What names?" snarled Sen. Robin Tut (R., Neb.).

"Perhaps these names will relieve the esteemed

Senator's patriotic doubts," said Benson Ruttenrib, a half smile curling his lips. "The signatories are: Terbin Neutron, B.S., renowned physicist and refuter of the Second Law of Thermodynamics; Sri Benur-Bonnett, the Anglo-Indian neutralist and doomsday prophet; R. T. Bun-Tsen Bernoi, the Eurasian Nobel Prize-winning chemist; Sr. Benite Bruntón, the former President of Cuba and ransomed Freedom Fighter; N. Robbinn Trustee, steel magnate, philanthropist, and beloved captain of industry; U Bronnerbet Sint, international peacemaker and Burmese diplomat; and, certainly last but by no means least, Ens. Ronn B. Trubite, America's most adored naval hero and currently the President of the United States!"

"Sound like a bunch of Commies," offered Sen. Robin Tut (R., Neb.), on awakening from a short doze.

"Let's have none of that!" Sen. Trentin Burbo reprimanded, banging his gavel. "Call the witness."

I arose and nervously advanced toward the stand, but as I did so I suddenly saw that Sir Bennett Broun, René Bons-Bruttin, Buster Binnerton, Toni N. Ten Rubbers, Tornbein Stubner, Robert St. Bunnien, and several others had also stood up and were trying to take the stand. There was a nasty scuffle; the witness chair was overturned, and a photographer's camera was trampled. Through the clamor, the staccato rapping of the gavel, and Sen. Trentin Burbo's shouts of "Let's have some orduh and decorum!," I heard the resonant voice of Benson Ruttenrib at my ear. "Plead the Fifth," he said simply.

Well, the worst is over now. All my friends will be glad to know I've been to a doctor, who has said it's really nothing to worry about, and that I should take a fairly long vacation or perhaps adopt an interesting hobby. As far as the doctor is concerned, I'm just about cured. He, by the way, is a top man who used to practice at Bethesda Naval Hospital. His name is Bob Tinner (USN, Ret.).

Songs of Fridtjof Nansen Land (Another Arcane Label First)

© 1971 by The New York Times Company. Reprinted by permission.

SIDE ONE

Band 1. *Malya Cliqot Fridtg*—The Cold Weather Is Sometimes Bothersome

With an average mean temperature of 6.5 degrees F., the inhabitants of Fridtjof Nansen Land often gather together during the long Arctic winter in the *strebta*, or community house, and mildly curse their birth with the glottal, dirgelike *"Malya Cliqot Fridtg."* The reference to Novaya Zemlya, a large island to the immediate south where the average mean temperature is 8.2 degrees F., is clearly envious.

BURTON BERNSTEIN

> *Sometimes the cold is too much to bear,*
> Malya Cliqot Fridtg,
> *And I wish to God I was born on sunny*
>   *Novaya Zemlya,*
> Malya malya cliqot fridtg,
> *Where the girls are known to laugh.*
> Malya malya malya cliqot.

Band 2. *Chaiya, Chaiya Zumer!*—Hail, Hail to Summer!

The four-day summer, arriving generally in the first week of August, is cause for much revelry. All work ceases and the islanders remove their *bruntas* (yakskin outer garments) so they can bathe their forearms in the gently melting snow. If, as sometimes happens, the sun breaks through, a worshipful pose is struck by the men, women and children. Then, forearms raised, they chant in unison:

> *Hail, hail to Summer!*
> *Season of no* bruntas,
> *When sky and heart are one*
> *And my arms are clean,*
> *And my arms are clean.*
> *Hail, hail to summer!*
> *The* zol *(sun) is on the snow*
> *And I've found at last my shadow,*
> *Who has clean arms, too,*
> *Who has clean arms, too.*
> Chaiya!

Band 3. *Giddap, Yak*—Giddap, Yak

The yak, a native hairy wild ox, is friend, clothier, family car, and larder to the Fridtjof Nansen Landsmen. Thus, it is impossible to overestimate the importance of the yakherd and his charges to the cultural life of the country. Is it any wonder, then, that every islander can

66

sing all 68 verses of the yakherder's lament? Verses 1 and 68 are sung here

> *Giddap, yak, giddap,*
> *I am cold, hungry and tired.*
> *On the fire in the* strebta
> *There is a stew of your brother,*
> *While my woman sews a* brunta
> > *from your mother.*
> *Giddap, yak, giddap,*
> *And let's go home.*

> *Giddap, yak, giddap,*
> *I am cold, hungry and tired.*
> *On the fire in the* strebta
> *There is a stew of your brother,*
> *While my woman sews a* brunta
> > *from your mother.*
> *Giddap, yak, giddap,*
> *And let's go home.*

Band 4. *Pichinyapzank*—The Trapper's Song

Next to yakherding, the chief occupation of the industrious Fridtjof Nansen Landsmen is trapping the indigenous fauna—bear, fox, ivory gulls and an occasional insect, usually the housefly. On nearby Novaya Zemlya, the wings of a fly will bring the fortunate trapper as much as 15 *drampas* during the tourist season (first week of August). So it is the rare fly that concerns the trapper most, not the more common, lichen-eating bear or fox.

> *Ah, little fly,*
> *I see you there upon the rock.*
> *Be still, my tiny friend,*
> *And I shall catch you.*

In the marketplace on nearby Novaya Zemlya
You will win me 15 drampas,
So I can buy a new sock for my beloved,
  for my beloved.
Be still, my tiny friend,
And I shall catch you.
Zwach! [*A sound made by slapping the open*
  hand against a Fridtjof Nansen Land rock.]

SIDE TWO
Band 1. *Hudtg Kalinka Hudtg*—More *Kalinka All Around*
  Kalinka, a kind of fermented yak milk, is the national beverage, and it is said that a quart downed at one sitting will put a grown man into a stupor for the entire winter. Around the *langstint* (long table) in the cozy *strebta*, this traditional drinking song may be heard on almost any given night, and often on into the next day. It is sung in repetitive chorus, until only one man is left upstanding. He then wanders out into the snow and is proclaimed mayor.

More kalinka *all around, boys,*
And drink your yak horns dry.
Tomorrow will be like today,
And today was very cold.
So more kalinka *all around, boys,*
More kalinka *all around.*

Band 2. *Nov Besya Ne Madl Wilczek*—How Pretty the Girls of Wilczek Land
  This plaintive ballad, usually sung by the men of Zichy Land, reflects a much deeper emotion than mere yearning for an allegedly fairer breed of woman. For two centuries, the males of Wilczek Land and Zichy Land have warred with each other over fly-trapping rights and the charms of their respective females. Careful examina-

tion of F.N.L. historical documents shows that nobody on either side has ever been injured during the Two Hundred Years' War, since both forces are sworn by blood oath never to step foot on each other's territory. However, feelings still run high whenever the subject is brought up.

Tell me not of girls from far-off climes
Where no yak has ever grazed,
For I have seen the Wilczek girls—
Every one a lovely,
Every one a queen.
How pretty the girls of Wilczek Land,
Fairer than my ugly Zichy woman.
Ah, what I would give to hold one near,
Except we are at war, except we are at war.
Alas, the snow is always whiter
On the other man's island.

Band 3. *Zhlifya, Zhlifya*—Sleep, Sleep
   There being no marked difference between day and night for 412 days of the Fridtjof Nansen Land year (the Fridtjof Nansen Land year has 416 days), the problem of the lullaby is a profound one. During the dark fall-winter-spring, children are frequently awake for as much as a whole week (about eight days), believing only one fun-filled day has passed. Then, lulled by the lurching motion of the mothers' ceremonial piggy-back, a half pint of cut *kalinka*, and general boredom, the tots fade into several weeks of insensibility, often to the strains of this tender air sung by the father or an uncle.

Zhlifya, zhlifya, zhlifya, zhlifya,
Zhlifya, zhlifya, zhlifya, zhlifya,
Go to sleep
Zhlifya, zhlifya, zhlifya, zhlifya,

Zhlifya, zhlifya, zhlifya, zhlifya,
Your mother's back is breaking.
Zhlifya, zhlifya, zhlifya, zhlifya,
Zhlifya, zhlifya, zhlifya, zhlifya,
It's a world you never made.

Band 4. *Jonkyi Dudl*—(No known translation)
The origin and meaning of this local ditty are vague, although many of the older islanders claim that Fridtjof Nansen himself created the tune when he first settled the archipelago during the discouraging winter of 1895. At any rate, the song has become an important part of the musical vernacular of the vast, grand land to which Fridtjof Nansen gave his name and his all.

Jonkyi Dudl wendya toyn,
Ryatink ena ponya,
Stukya fidtya endiskep
Ontkaldtya macaronya.

Look, Ma, I Am Kool!

By permission of Burton Bernstein. © 1977 Burton Bernstein.

[*EDITOR'S NOTE: The tragic passing of Al P. Wena, the young, opaque avant-garde playwright who died in a mysterious incident at the New York Botanical Garden, has left the shocked off-off-Broadway world with a serious talent vacuum. However, fortunately, friends of Mr. Wena, while sifting through his effects in his Avenue B loft, discovered a new play, written with red Magic Marker on a six-by-four-foot mirror. This work—which we print below in its entirety, before its forthcoming pro- duction—apparently stresses an earlier Wena theme, being an astringent comment on a loveless society's*

BURTON BERNSTEIN

extraordinary ability to overcommunicate. It would also seem to reflect Wena's mystical preoccupation with word games, particularly palindromes.]

LOOK, MA, I AM KOOL!
A New Play by Al P. Wena

Rota A'tor

E. FINK, a knife

"RATS" REPUS, superstar

XERXES, sex rex

LAERTES S., asset real

WOP, a P.O.W.

MADAM ADAM

TULSA, a slut

HANNAH

TUNA, a nut

YOGA, a goy

SIVA, a rara avis

OTTO
ABBA
ARA   signori, iron G.I.'s
GOG
RADAR

POP
MOM
SIS

("Llama's Eyes," a mall)

> E. FINK, a knife
>
Egad! Lo, old age.

> LAERTES S., asset real
>
St. Eliot et al made E. dam late toilets.

> "RATS" REPUS, superstar
>
He said, *"Dias,"* eh?

> RADAR
>
O.K. to T.K.O.?

> "RATS" REPUS, superstar
>
Not now, Wonton.

> E. FINK, a knife
>
(E. faces soup) Pousse-café!

> TULSA, a slut
>
(Straps E.'s parts)
>
Liar! Smart as a tram's rail.

E. FINK, a knife

(E. waxes, sex awe)
Noiseless, a timed step,
Sees pet's demitasse.
Lesion!

(Dog's awe: E. was God)

OTTO
Oho!

ARA
Aha!

SIVA, a rara avis
Peep peep.

GOG
Tut-tut.

RADAR
Yap, yap, yap. Pay, pay, pay.

("Zeus' Nimrod," a dorm in Suez)

ABBA
Viva le tide di Tel Aviv!

YOGA, a goy
Viva let live! Evil Tel Aviv.

MADAM ADAM
(Drol' as a lord)
Viva! Let live evil Tel Aviv!

YOGA, a goy
A hairy son sees no Syria. Ha!

ABBA
Nu, U.N.?

WOP, a P.O.W.
War *è* raw.

"RATS" REPUS, superstar
(Re: wop power)
Nail a timid god on rood. Door no dog, dim Italian.

WOP, a P.O.W.
O, nail a Titan! Nat, Italiano.
Up ante, Etna. P.U.!

TULSA, a slut
(Level as a ... level)
O, gnat — a tango!

OTTO
Mit Tim?

BURTON BERNSTEIN

WOP, a P.O.W.

(Wolfs a raga in Niagara's flow)
    Amor!
    Oil gig!
    A sip!
    On, Rovil!
    O to Livorno, Pisa, Giglio, Roma!

LAERTES S., asset real

Drab bard.

"RATS" REPUS, superstar

Gulp a slab o' balsa plug!

SIGNORI, IRON G.I.'s

Hush, suh.

(Moor deb's bedroom)

XERXES, sex rex

En giro torte sol ciclos et rotor igne.

RADAR

(Nips rotor spin)
    Harris on Radar? No sirrah.

HANNAH

Sagas on Hannah? No sagas.

(Stinker Hannah reknits)

    XERXES, sex rex
Air à la Maia — malaria.

    ARA
 Yo batta. Atta boy!

    ABBA
A nest, a nest! *Tsena, tsena!*

    OTTO
Gog, am I Magog?

    GOG
Gog am Magog!

    E. FINK, a knife
(Cased Lucy by cul-de-sac)
 Re: drums. It is murder.

    "RATS" REPUS, superstar
If I had a hi-fi...

    POP
(Elk nite tinkle)
 Elay! Elay! Elay! Yale! Yale! Yale!

>   E. FINK, a knife
> Puerile Eli, re-up!

>   POP
> Swap paws?

>   SIS
> Hey, Dad, yeh!

>   E. FINK, a knife
> *(E. gats stage)*
> No gnus is... I sung on.

>   TULSA, a slut
> *(Stops E.'s pots)*
> No gnus have evah sung on.

>   MOM
> *(Toped at a depot)*
> Th' gin 'ot', please. E.'s a 'elp tonight.

(Enter ret'n'e)

>   XERXES, sex rex
> *(Draws a sward)*
> E. Fink won a "now" knife.

TUNA, a nut
Switchblade... Na! An edalbhctiws.

SIGNORI, IRON G.I.s
Shush, suhs.

WOP, a P.O.W.
'At'sa *basta.*

MARSHALL BRICKMAN

What, Another Legend?

Reprinted by permission; © 1973 The New Yorker
Magazine, Inc.

*Trans-Ethnic Gesellschaft is pleased to announce the
release of another album in its Geniture series of record-
ings devoted to giants in American jazz. These liner
notes are by the noted jazz critic and historian Arthur
Mice, whose efforts first brought Pootie LeFleur to
public attention.*

Pootie LeFleur, a legendary figure in the development of
American jazz, was discovered—or *re*discovered, rather
—last summer placidly raking leaves on the courthouse
lawn in Shibboleth, Louisiana. Although one hundred

and twelve years old and in semiretirement (two days a week, he drops paper bags of water from his second-story window onto passersby below, for which he receives a small sum), Pootie has astonishing powers of recall, displaying the lucidity of a man easily fifteen years his junior. On a recent visit engendered by the production of this record, we got Pootie talking about the roots of the music he knows so well.

"Was there an ideal period when jazz was pure, untainted by any influence foreign to its African origins?" we asked.

"I spec'... um... *rebesac*, dey's a *flutterbug*, hee, hee, hee!" Pootie said, squinting very hard and making a popping sound with his teeth.

"And what of the blues? Don't the blues, with their so-called 'blue notes,' represent a significant deviation from standard European tonality?"

"I'se ketch a ravis, y'heah? A ravis, an' de *dawg,* he *all* onto a *runnin'* boa'd," replied the jazz great, leaning back in his chair expansively until his head touched the floor.

This album represents the distillation of over sixty hours of taped conversations with Pootie LeFleur (of which the above is but a fragment), plus all the significant available recorded performances by this authentic primitive genius, whose career spanned the entire jazz era, from Jelly Roll Morton to John Coltrane—including a three-month hiatus in 1903, when nobody in New Orleans could seem to get in tune.

Carlyle Adolph Bouguereau "Pootie" LeFleur was born into the fertile musical atmosphere of postbellum New Orleans. His mother had favorably impressed Scott Joplin by playing ragtime piano with her thighs, and his father was a sometime entrepreneur, who once owned the lucrative ad-lib franchise for all of Storyville and the north delta; for years, no New Orleans musician could shout "Yeh, daddy!" during or after a solo without paying Rebus LeFleur a royalty. The young boy taught himself to play the piano with some help from his uncle, the legendary "Blind" (Deaf) Wilbur MacVout, for two decades a trombonist with Elbert Hubbard, although Hubbard was an author and had no real need for a trombonist. When Pootie was five, he was given his own piano but misplaced it, requiring him to practice thereafter on the dining-room table.[1]

When Pootie was six, the LeFleur home was razed to make way for a bayou, and Pootie's father made the decision to relocate the family in St. Louis. Here Pootie tried his hand at composition. "The Most Exceedin' Interestin' Rag," the first effort which we have in manuscript, is clearly an immature conception; only two measures long, it contains a curious key signature indicated by a very large sharp accidental over the treble clef, and a flat and a half-moon drawn in the bass. The piece is melodically sparse (the entire tune consists of one whole note, with a smiling face drawn in it), but it does anticipate Pootie's characteristic economy by at least a decade. The material from this period (some of which is also available on "Pre-Teen Pootie," 12" Trans-Ethnic Gesellschaft TD 203) reveals a profusion of styles and influences. "Spinoza's Joy" has a definite Spanish, if not Sephardic, flavor, while "What Vous Say?" shows a hint of the Creole.

According to Dr. Ernst Freitag and Gustav Altschuler's encyclopedic Dictionary of Jazz and Home Wiring Simplified (Miffin Verlag, 1942), the next few years were ones of extreme financial deprivation for the LeFleurs. Pootie's father had squandered the family

---

[1]Johnny St. Cyr recalled an anecdote about Pootie's habit of playing out scales and figures on the table. One night in 1938, Pootie, Kid Ory, Baby Dodds, and Tiny Grimes were at Small's Paradise having a late supper of miniature gherkins, and Pootie was occupied as usual tapping out a riff with his right hand. It finally became too much for Ory, and the famous tailgater put down his fork. "Stop that, Pootie," said the Kid. "It's annoying." Although attributed to many others, including Fletcher Henderson and Dorothy Parker, the remark was in fact made by Ory.

savings by investing in a feckless enterprise called Fin-Ray Cola, a tuna-flavored soft drink, and in an attempt to bring in some money Pootie invented a new note, located between F and F sharp, which he named "Reep," and tried peddling it door to door. Despite early bad luck, Pootie never lost faith in "my fine new note," as he called it, and some time later he hired a hall in Sedalia to test public reaction and attract financial backing. The playing of the note apparently made no impression on the casual Missourians, most of whom arrived too late to hear it.

It was about this time that LeFleur played for James P. Johnson, who urged him to go to New York or any other city a thousand miles away. The story of that trip is probably the most fascinating in the entire history of jazz, but unfortunately Pootie claims to have forgotten it. By now a leader and innovator in his own right, Pootie organized himself and three other musicians into what Nat Hentoff has called a "quartet," and secured an engagement at Buxtehude's, a speakeasy in the heart of Manhattan's swinging Flemish district. His first wife, singer Rubella Cloudberry, evokes those exciting years in her autobiography, "A Side of Fries" (Snead House, Boston, 1951):

> Well, don't you know, Pootie come in one night and say, "Pack up, woman, we goin' to the Big Apple!" And I say, "Hunh?" And so he say, "Pack up, woman, we goin' to the Big Apple!" And I say, "The big what?" So we stayed in Chicago.[2]

The stimulating, rough-and-tumble atmosphere of Prohibition sparked LeFleur's group (the Mocha Jokers) and others to marvellous feats of improvisation, typified by the moment during one dinner show at Tony Pastor's

---

[2]Of course, when LeFleur did make it to New York it was without his saxophonist, Crazy Earl Bibbler. Two days before the trip, Bibbler, an alcoholic, sold his lips to a pawnshop for twenty dollars.

when Bix Beiderbecke blew a brilliant version of "Dardanella" on a roast chicken.[3]

LeFleur's classical period begins with the reflective "Boogie for the Third Sunday After Epiphany" and ends with the tender and haunting "Toad" Nocturne. "Toad" opens with a simple piano motif in G, which is reworked into C, F, F minor, and B, finally retiring to E flat to freshen up. At the very end, following a tradition as old as the blues, everybody stops playing.

One of the hallmarks of LeFleur's career was his constant effort to adapt his style to contemporary trends —with the result that he was habitually accused of plagiarism. When the New Orleans style (or "Chicago style," as it was then called) waned, Pootie was eclipsed, but he reappears in 1939 as a member of the historic Savoy Sextet sessions, featuring Bird, Diz, Monk, Prez, and Mrs. Hannah Weintraub on vibes.[4] With a penchant for overstatement typical of the period, Pootie tried augmenting the sextet, changing it first into a septet, then an octet, then a nonet, a dectet, an undectet, and so on, ending up with the cumbersome "hundred-tet," which could only be booked into meadows. A major influence on him at this time was his attendance at a tradition-breaking rent-party jam session, during which nineteen consecutive choruses of "How High the Moon" were played in twelve seconds by "Notes" Gonzales— the brilliant and erratic disciple of Charlie Parker—who was later killed when his car crashed into the tower of the Empire State Building.

The next album in this series will cover Pootie's modern period, including the prophetic Stockholm concert, with Ornette Coleman on vinyl sax and Swedish reedman Bo Ek on Dacron flute, plus some very recent sides cut by Pootie at his own expense in the Record-Your-Voice booth at the West Side bus terminal in New York City.

[3] As retold by Miff Mole.

[4] Hear especially the second take of "Schizoroonia on Hannah Banana —The Flip Side of Mrs. Weintraub" (Ulysses 906) for a remarkable polytonal chord cluster achieved when her necklace broke.

GORDON COTLER

Name Tag

By permission of Gordon Cotler. Copyright 1969
Gordon Cotler.

Done! That's it. You really rode those grooves for the
wrap-up. This last hour was on the jet stream all the
way. How cunning not to have knocked off at bedtime.
What happened to that theory that after 2 A.M. a kind of
fault line opens somewhere in the brain and the work
goes lopsided? Pushing on to the end tonight was a
master stroke of intuition. You went through that last
chapter like the Super Chief through Widgetville. What
an outline! Massive, dense, inevitable—as awesome as
the bulk and movement of a Canadian glacier. Fellah,
you're going to have yourself a novel! The book clubs

will be sniffing under your study window as you pull the last sheet from the machine; the movie prowls will spring from the bushes. And not a single false note, not a millimeter of concession, anywhere in the *oeuvre*, to the marketplace.

But can you write it? Can you *afford* to write it? There are years of dog work ahead. Take Part One, where you survey the financial woes of the Union during the closing weeks of the Civil War, from inside the head of Salmon P. Chase. That chunk alone, what with the time needed to research the frame of reference of a pre-Keynesian economist, his vocabulary, and all—to say nothing of the family picture, ferreting out his secret life, if he had one—should take you a good year. A year, easy. And that's nothing to Part Three, where the reader will see the supply problems of the Seventh Cavalry in the late seventies through the eyes of Rapid Bear, a Choctaw quartermaster clerk raised by evangelized Piutes. What kind of hangups, for instance, was Rapid Bear likely to have in the hay, or the long grass, or wherever it was Choctaws tangled to release their tensions when they slipped out of the tepee? Or was it a hogan? See what I mean? You've got six months of nosey-Parkering right there.

Face it. You want to feed the wife and kids these next three years, not to mention keeping up your own strength, you're going to need a foundation grant. A jumbo. Play it smart and start at the top—the Ford Foundation! Wasn't old Henry mad for America's youth? And is any story more rail-splittingly American than yours? The Ford Foundation will come across with a fistful of the crisp. Shoot a letter out first thing in the morning, and be sure to go right to the president. Lay out your dream for his personal inspection.

Why wait for morning? It's barely a quarter to four. Write the letter now, while the sap is running. The foundation's address will be in the Manhattan book.

Sure, here it is. Slip this sheet of letterhead into the old machine and talk to it.

Mr. George McBundy
The Ford Foundation
477 Madison Avenue
New York, N.Y.

Dear Mr. McBundy:

Wait a sec. That doesn't look right. Is "Foundation" misspelled? No, it's the name, the president's name. Actually, it's something off-beat. Not George McBundy, but Bundy McGeorge. Something like that. McBund Georgy? McGeorge Bundy? Bund McGeorgy?

Stop. Stop and visualize. You've seen that name just in the last day or two, in the *Times.* Try to picture it. An inside page, left-hand side, third or fourth paragraph of a full column piece. A local story by McPhillips Candlish, Philip McCandlish. Candlish McPhilips? Phyllis McCandles. It doesn't matter. Concentrate on the *shape* of the name. The "Mc" makes it into a triple name, sort of. Like that actress, that thin blond one—Eva St. Marie. Ava St. Marie? Eva St. Agnes? *Stop.* Come in off that tangent. McBund Georgy.

It will come. It's only four-fifteen. Write a draft of the letter. By the time it's ready to type out clean the name will have popped up. George Bundy. Never mind. Focus on the letter. What do you want to say? How to convey the epic sweep of this fiscal-military cavalcade? Maybe it would be wise to begin in a remote corner of the story, with one determined man's dream of the single tax—George Henry brooding on his own grinding poverty in a flourishing land. George Henry? Here we go again. John Henry? No, John Henry is the steel-drivin' man. George is right, that part is right. George Sand? George Sanders? George Sand Marie?

This is grotesque. Forget the letter. Concentrate

for a moment on getting some names straight. Any names. Once you get into the rhythm of it, the block will dissolve. Start with a simple name. Harry S. Truman. There, that's better. Harry Truman, Bess Truman, Margaret Truman. It gets easier. Margaret's husband down at the *Times*—Daniel Clifton. Cliff Danielson. Bundy McGeorge.

Four-thirty-five. Go to sleep. Who are you kidding? You'll never sleep now. Finish roughing out your letter; the name will take care of itself. Concentrate on the letter. Build your presentation backward and outward from the dream of the single tax to the budgeting, in Part Three, of the Mexican War. Suggest how you will follow the *Sturm und Drang* from inside the noggin of Scott Winfield's paymaster. Is that Winfield Scott? No, Scott Winfield, as in Holden Caulfield. Winfield Scott only sounds right because of *Dred* Scott.

Ten minutes to five. Why don't you black out and start again, *tabula rasa*, after a hot breakfast? Baloney. You wouldn't sleep now under chloroform. McBund Georgy, George McBundy. Georgie Bundy. Beulah Bondi. Eva St. Marie. How about opening the letter with, "President, The Ford Foundation. My Dear Sir...."? Never. You can't write a To Whom It May Concern letter when you're asking two hundred bucks a week walking-around money, plus a couple of thou to fly west and explore the psychic bonds that connect Choctaw and Piute. George McBond.

All right. Just sit there and get a grip on yourself. Say names. Say hard names. Go on. Bethel Leslie. Why Bethel Leslie? Leslie Howard. Howard Hughes. Hughes Rudd. Rudd Weatherwax. Who the hell is Rudd Weatherwax? He's Leslie's trainer, that's who. I mean, Lassie's trainer. Come on, fellah, if you can say Lassie's trainer's name you can say anyone's. Eva Marie Saint. Eva Marie Saint—that's it! George McBundy. Ford McHenry. George

Macready. George Reedy. McGuffey T. Reader. George B. McUndy.

    Five o'clock. Why don't you wake the wife? She has to get up anyway in an hour or two to see the kids off to school. Don't you dare. That's out. But if she *happens* to be awake, why not ask her?

    "Honey, are you awake? Are you up?"

    "Huh?"

    "I just wanted to know, what's the name of the president of the Ford Foundation?"

    "What? Did you say something?"

    "The president of the Ford Foundation. What's his name?"

    "McGeorge Bundy."

    "You're no help. Go to sleep."

    Their switchboard won't open till nine. Ten, in that kind of organization. Wait a minute. There's a brother! I can pinpoint him through the brother. I'm sure there's a brother, in the State Department. William McBundy! Bundy McWilliams. *Carey* McWilliams? Leo McCarey. McBond Georgy. Who else can I wake?

My Stay in an American Hospital

Copyright 1973 *Saturday Review*. Reprinted by permission.

(The following was dispatched today to the People's Republic of China by Li Chin Tao, the newly accredited American correspondent of the Peking Evening Star*)*

My three-day stay at an American hospital has ended, and now I can share this curious adventure with my readers. The story begins on my very first day in New York, when, on the recommendation of a colleague, I chose to dine at a restaurant that features a typical American fare known as "Pailful of Chicken." To understand what befell me that evening, it is necessary to attempt a description of the bizarre yet savory concoction that makes up virtually the entire menu of such eating places. Picture, if you will, the morsels of chicken encountered in ordinary cooking assembled somehow into the approximate shape of wing, breast, or leg such as is encountered on the sentient fowl of yard or farm. The construction is no more noxious-looking than it may seem in the reading, and the flavor excuses all.

The more squeamish among my readers might want to skip to the next paragraph. To insure that the chicken as served in this recipe keeps the original chicken shape, the bird's skeletal substructure must be retained in the cooking. A piece of this bone matter lodged in my throat. Within moments the discomfort became so intense that only by concentrating on our Chairman's admonition to recall, in times of adversity, a worse circumstance with which we are acquainted, was I able to retain some semblance of equilibrium. I thought of the mother of my wife, who, during the building of the Hankow Road, was pinned for seventeen hours under a lorry filled with pea gravel, and the pain eased a bit.

Fortunately, the ambulance was not long in coming, and in the interim every effort was made to put me at my ease. I was laid out on the floor of the restaurant, and the other diners rearranged their chicken pails so that they faced away from my prostrate body, thus reducing my embarrassment. The restaurant owner loosened my necktie, for which I was grateful, and disturbed me barely at all when he extracted from the wallet in my jacket and from a trouser pocket the two dollars and forty-seven cents for the food I had caused to have prepared for me. A moment later a waxed-paper sack containing those segments of chicken I had not had the opportunity to eat was placed on my stomach, and a solicitous waiter crouched to shout in my ear that

I could take this with me to consume at my leisure. A moment after that I was lifted into the ambulance.

The hospital proved to be a large, modern plant, and the tracheotomy was performed by a medical team of high professional standards and unexceptionable skills. Only one incident out of the ordinary occurred, and this bears reporting. A needle was inserted near the site of the impending incision, and I assumed this was the start of anesthesia. I could not have been more wrong: this was *all* of it! No further needles were inserted and, almost instantly, this one was *removed*. Difficult as the assertion might be to accept, it must be reported that all pain soon disappeared. There was no further discomfort and, in point of fact, I found myself conversing and even exchanging jokes with the attendant doctors and nurses. A day or two later I made a point of inquiring about this remarkable anesthesia. I was told I had been administered a "local anesthetic." If one patient's complete satisfaction is any indication, it will not long remain local! Indeed, it ill-behooves our own establishment not to loosen the blinders that keep it on the path of generally accepted practice and well back from the frontiers of medical exploration, no matter how unorthodox the routes.

During the ensuing days of recuperation, I took advantage of my situation to make some notes on American hospital practice. *Item*: None of the rooms on my floor were furnished with more than four beds, and some had as few as one! Discreet inquiries revealed that this "shortage of hospital beds" is nationwide. So much for the "marketplace" American economy's reputed ability to adjust to the needs of the populace, its so-called flexibility to produce items that are much in demand! Sunglasses are in such profusion here that they are stacked ten high on drugstore counters. In a

GORDON COTLER

frantic effort to consume this overproduction they are worn buried in the hair or in dimly lighted rooms. But since there is no central planning, factories that might be converted to the manufacture of needed hospital beds still mindlessly spew forth sunglasses.

Item: At hospital meal times, great effort went into serving all parts of meals, from soup to ice cream, exactly at room temperature, neither warmer nor cooler. Does some vestige of superstition, some folk-medicine hangover in the U.S. medical establishment, encourage the belief that this quaint practice speeds patient recovery?

Item: Upon discharge from the hospital I became privy to a delightful practice. Departing patients are presented a sheet of foolscap on which is itemized the various services that were performed, each followed by a dollar figure approximating the capital expenditure behind the service. For example, my "bill," as it is called, told me how much it had cost to educate the surgeon who operated on me, the construction cost of the room in which I was housed, the price of the machine that took my X-ray pictures, and so on. The "bill" serves both as a souvenir of what happened during one's hospital stay, and as useful instruction on how great a drain of the nation's wealth is the effort to keep its citizens healthy—a none-too-subtle reminder to cooperate with medical authorities in that effort! On leaving, I expressed my deep-felt appreciation of the "bill" to various staff members, and sensed, from the expression on their faces rather than from their words, how moved they were at my understanding of this touching document.

So, once again, thanks to the thoroughly efficient and modern American medical establishment, I am up and about, and pursuing my duties.

Tomorrow: How to open a "charge account" at a New York savings bank.

96

GERALD JONAS

The Mystery of the Purloined Grenouilles (A Tale of Ratiocinative Science Fiction)

Copyright © 1966 by Mercury Press, Inc. From *The Magazine of Fantasy and Science Fiction.*

BREKEKE-KEX KOAX KOAX
   —Aristophanes

Ratiocination is, in itself, a science. This basic truth (on which I often ruminate) invariably brings to mind a curious occurrence which I offer here by way of illustration of the proposition advanced in the first sentence of this somewhat circuitous paragraph.

It was toward the latter portion of April in the year 19— that I made the reacquaintance of a certain M. Edouard W—, whose agility of thought had most favorably impressed me during a brief *rencontre* in his rooms at 14 Rue Auber in the Weir section of the 15th *Arondissement* of P— many years ago. A man of noble parentage but sadly diminished means, he had lately retired to his ancestral home on the North Shore of L— I—, where he supplemented his meager "second income" by some discreet winkle picking. When, therefore, he called me long distance from his desolate *pied-à-mer* to urge attendance on his unhappy fate, I felt compelled to undertake the journey, arduous though it may be during rush hour.

I arrived just as a sun of immense orange girth was settling into the salty water behind his seedy house. Darkness comes swiftly on the North Shore, and the house was quite submerged in gloom when my friend opened the door; yet I could make out the tension that held his perfectly shaped nostrils in thrall. Settled at length on a *chaise longue* in his kitchen, I begged him to tell me without delay what was up.

"You will no doubt remember," he began, in a *patois* that bespoke both the 15th *Arondissement* and the 516 Area Code, "the work on electromagnetism brought to fruition by Professor Luigi Galvani of Bologna before his untimely death. Through experimentation, he established that an electrical current introduced into the leg of a member of the genus *Batrachia*—even one recently deceased—will result in a muscular spasm roughly proportional to the strength of the electrical impulse and the dimensions of the frog's leg. The principle he gave his life for—he died some years ago of a severe case of warts—is now, like nuclear physics and DNA, the intellectual property of every schoolchild. However, by applying the techniques of ratiocination, I only recently made the startling discovery that the true significance of Galvani's work has not yet been plumbed!"

Bursting with justifiable curiosity, I here interposed a question that had been forming in my mind from the very beginning of this bizarre recital: "What," I asked, "is that awful smell?"

W— coughed gently, and then (with a little nod of his perfectly shaped head as if to suggest that a gentleman of reduced means could not be held accountable for every little stink on L— I—) he went on:

"Ratiocination is, in itself, a science. For in what, essentially, does Reason consist if not in the process of ratiocination itself? Thus, by a simple infarction of the principle of *non sequitur*, I concluded that by reversing the procedure of Galvani it might be possible to produce massive quantities of electromagnetical energies, at a substantial savings over the rates of the L— I— Lighting Company. You may observe on the kitchen table the results of my labors."

Peering as closely as I dared at the tabletop, I immediately espied a number of copper wires leading from a number of tightly bound copper coils to a number of small plates of some porcelain-like material. On the plates themselves, where I had already guessed the key to the experiment should lie, there was absolutely— nothing!

Aghast, I whirled about to confront my friend, but the delicate smile on his perfectly shaped lips told me what I should have already known: i.e., that he already knew. "Indeed," he began, "the frogs are gone. It is as you see every morning. I import from P— at great expense a number of frogs—members of the noble species *Rana esculenta*. After linking them up to dynamos, I begin to tickle them gently with this goose feather you perceive here. The frogs begin to laugh, their legs twitch with uncontrollable glee, and great waves of galvanic energy surge back through the copper wires into the copper coils. From thence comes the power that lights my lights, heats my heat, and operates the few appliances in my humble home. The frogs—chosen for their abundance of Batrachian risibility as well as the development of their leg muscles—continue to chuckle all night, and this provides just enough current to power a tiny night-light beside my workbench. When I awake—but what do I say that you have not already guessed?—when I awake, prepared to stir my house to life again with a waft of a goose feather, I find that the frogs have quite—vanished!"

I shuddered uncontrollably. It was not yet summer on L— I—, and there are uncharted winds on that North Shore that blow with an almost Arctic ferocity. The lightless, heatless house seemed colder suddenly, and I noticed for the first time, staring at my hapless friend, the perfectly shaped bags beneath his eyes. "Your phone," I said, lifting the receiver, "is not powered by your homemade generator?" My deduction proved to be correct, and without waiting for confirmation, I dialed the number of my other good friend, Jules D—P—, who had only recently emigrated to this country to assume direction of a Belgian-waffle concession on M— Avenue.

As quickly, briefly, simply, and concisely as I was able, I outlined the situation to him, after which he said, "Do not disturb anything. Do not move, except for calls of nature and perhaps an occasional snack. You may open one window, but that only in the kitchen and on the leeward side. I shall be there in one hour and twelve minutes, unless today is Saturday, Sunday or a holiday, in which case I must allow six minutes more to change at J—."

I assured him that it was Tuesday, and, some thirty seconds before the appointed time, we perceived a knock on the door. But when my friend W— went to unlatch it, there was no one to be seen. The threshold was—empty! Precisely thirty seconds later, a shadowy figure appeared in the leeward window frame and let itself into the kitchen. It resolved itself into my friend D—P—. "The mystery is resolved," he said quietly.

"But how..." I began.

"Ratiocination is, in itself, a science," he began,

so quickly after I myself had begun that I was forced to put an end, however temporarily, to my beginning. "You, W—, are a somnambulist," D—P— went on. "This is evident from the bags, however well-shaped they may be, under your bloodshot eyes. Also, your funds are low, as evidenced by the fact that your house is bare of most of the accustomed amenities but a winkle-picking rake, a night-light, two *chaises longues*, and a few *anciens* appliances that I stepped over while climbing in. Ergo, we need look no further for a culprit, *mon cher* W—, than you yourself! Nightly you arise from your uneasy rest, haunted by dreams of your former riches, and pass into the kitchen where, by the meager glow of the night-light, your eyes cannot fail to discern the faintly chuckling amphibians on the dinner plates on the kitchen table. Being of Gallic mind and body, your unconscious is not only ratiocinative but eminently pragmatic, and it instantly constructs a hypothesis linking the emptiness of your stomach, the function of table and plates, and the sight of the succulent *grenouilles*."

"In other words..." I began.

"*Mais oui*," D—P— riposted. "When W— finishes his secret repast, he unconsciously seeks a way to clear the debris. But his unconscious, which is after all *not* conscious, cannot be expected to remember that, without frogs, this house has no electrical power and that, ergo, the electrically operated garbage-disposal unit, indigenous to all houses on this Shore, cannot operate. If I am correct in my chain of deductions—and I am— you will find in the kitchen sink both the evidence for the resolution of this mystery and the explanation for that ghastly stench you now perceive."

With a thin, high-pitched wail that sounded like a logician *in extremis*, W— raced to the kitchen sink. We followed hard on his heels. There, in a jumbled heap of frog bones and gristle, could be seen an unutterably liquescent mass of glaucous and nacreous—leftovers! *In pace requiescat.*

GARRISON KEILLOR

Local Family Keeps Son Happy

Reprinted by permission; © 1970 The New Yorker
Magazine, Inc.

What happens when parents buy a woman for their sixteen-year-old son? Even in this "swinging" age, such an arrangement would seem to violate most commonly held moral standards. Not so, say Mr. and Mrs. Robert Shepard, of 1417 Swallow Lane.

Two months ago, the Shepards obtained the parole of a twenty-four-year-old prostitute from the County Detention Farm. The woman came to work for the Shepards as a live-in companion for their son, Robert, Jr.

"Robbie had seemed restless and unhappy all last

summer," says Mrs. Shepard, a short, neat woman. "He was too young to get a job, and we were afraid he would take up drugs or smoking and drinking. We didn't want him staying out late with the car and taking part in reckless activities. We thought it would be safer to give him what all boys want."

The woman, whose name is Dorothy, is a shapely brunette who could easily pass for eighteen.

"Our boy has matured greatly in the few short weeks since Dorothy came to work for us," says Mr. Shepard, 48, who is an electronics engineer. "He is more poised and more relaxed."

"We see more of him this way, since he stays home evenings and weekends," adds Mrs. Shepard.

Despite the Shepards' success with Dorothy, none of their neighbors have bought women for their sons. For one thing, the cost is prohibitive for many families; Dorothy's wages come to $75 per week, plus room and board.

How does Robbie feel about his new friend?

"At first, I was nervous and keyed-up," he says. "I didn't know what to expect. Gradually, I got used to it and settled down."

In addition to her other duties, Dorothy also cooks breakfast. One of her specialties is fancy eggs.

FANCY EGGS
6 eggs
1 cup chopped onion
½ cup chopped green pepper
1 cup tomato sauce

Fry the eggs over easy. Before the eggs become firm, add onion and green pepper. Pour tomato sauce over the eggs and season to taste. Serve hot with corn bread and coffee.

Your Wedding and You: A Few Thoughts on Making It More Personally Rewarding, Shared by Reverend Bob Osman

TO HOWIE, CHRIS, LANI, KIM, STEVE, GREG, SANDI, CAROL, JIM, JAKI, AND ALL THE YOUNG PEOPLE WHO TAUGHT ME TO LOVE THEM.

Reprinted by permission; © 1975 The New Yorker Magazine, Inc.

In the gentle happy mornin'
Of the country love we've known,
Let's build a life together
And make ourselves at home.

—Jack Aspen

Cherry Tree Music, Inc.
Used by permission. Made in U.S.A.
All rights reserved.
Courtesy of
THE HUNDRED FLOWERS BRIDAL SHOP
Designers—Consultants—Caterers
"We Care"

In the past decade, a very rapidly increasing change in our views of marriage as an institution and the wedding ceremony as an expression of two persons' feelings about marriage and about themselves and each other, their place in the community and society, and their relationship to the planet itself (and, of course, God) has undoubtedly taken place. Perhaps this change is summed up fairly well by two young people whom I'll call *Pat* and *Mike.*

"People like us reject the stereotypes, the role-playing, that seem to be so much a part of other people's relationships," they confided to me one day during pre-marital counselling. "We are individuals with an infinite capacity for loving, sharing, knowing, caring, growing, and expanding. We want our wedding to express that unique personalness, that *beingness*, that each of us, and only us, can bring to marriage. Do you know what we mean?"

More and more, most of us do—especially those in the 18-to-35 age group in which most first marriages take place. Oftentimes writing their own ceremonies and creating their own symbols, language, music, feelings, this generation of young couples is seeking new modes, new marriage styles, to express what one minister called "the naturally religious, the realistically mystical, the practically impossible."

Heavy, right?

Not necessarily. In fact, the emphasis is definitely *away* from heaviness and *toward* lightness and informality. Comfortable. Feeling good. Being yourself. Being okay.

That is what the "New Wedding" is all about.

What is the "New Wedding"?
Okay, let's get down to specifics.
First of all, the New Wedding is less likely to

occur in a formal place of worship or government but, rather, in an environment where the couple feels comfortable—a natural hillside or valley, a favorite restaurant, a nearby park or playground, or the home of a close friend.

Second, it is less likely to involve formal Judeo-Christian-establishment language but, rather, words that the couple would want to say to each other even if they weren't getting married.

Third, it is more likely to make each person attending the ceremony feel like a participant in something that is very interesting indeed.

Of course, many couples still elect a more traditional ceremony: the white tunics and daisy crowns, the lighting of matches by the congregation, the beautiful Peter, Paul and Mary songs, and such a ceremony can be deeply meaningful in its own way. Certainly no couple should reject it just to be "different." An Alternative Wedding should be chosen only after careful and sincere discussion of the couple's own values, dreams, and aptitudes at this most important moment in their life.

What is an "Alternative Wedding"?
That's a good question. I'd say, "It depends pretty much on the individual," so let's look at some individual cases.

Sam and *Judy*, for example. They chose to emphasize their mutual commitment to air and water quality, exchanging vows while chained to each other and to the plant gate of a major industrial polluter.

Lyle and *Marcia*, recognizing their dependence on each other, were joined in matrimony in a crowd of total strangers and had but $3.85 and a couple of tokens between them.

Al and *Tammy*, on the other hand, sharing a commitment to challenge and excitement, were married in 6.12 seconds in *Al's* Supercharged Funny Car, with a minister on her lap and four bridesmaids on the floor (a new track record).

Bud and *Karen* chose a simple ceremony in their own apartment, with *Karen* fixing pizza in the kitchen, *Bud* asleep on the sofa, and their *two children* throwing toys at the guests.

Charles and *Frank*, however, selected the Early Traditional style, complete with morning coats, Wagner and Mendelssohn, and crustless sandwiches.

Others have been married in canoes or small powerboats, under bridges, in tunnels, beside creeks, on towers, over the telephone (with the groom calling from a distant tavern), and on ski tows, islands, mountain peaks, peninsulas, rooftops, and rocks. A New, or Alternative, Wedding means freedom to be married in exactly the way you always wanted to be.

What is an "Alternative, or New, Wedding"?

Very well, let's look at three basic elements of the marriage ceremony in terms of personal experience today: readings, or literature; ceremony itself, or drama; and singing, or music. All are forms of *celebration*, from the Latin word *"celebratio,"* meaning "to get along famously, or quickly."

MUSIC. The music of Scott Joplin, Bob Dylan, Barbra Streisand, the Carpenters, the Grateful Dead, "Sesame Street," Pepsi-Cola, and the Fifties is often chosen, though many couples are now creating their own music. *Henry* and *Phyllis* were members of the Beloveds, a bliss-rock band, and decided to hold their wedding in a large auditorium, with a sellout crowd sharing the joy and excitement of a Beloveds concert. Although the band had never played outside of small coffeehouses and was little known on the music scene, with the help and concern of a supportive promoter the concert was arranged, with ticket prices scaled upward accordingly. "It was a wonderful wedding, and we all got off on it, especially the aspect of total sharing," remarked *Phyllis* afterward. "And there would've been even more to share, except the promoter took sixty per cent off the top, and expenses wiped out the rest. Which goes to show the importance of having a good wedding contract." Alternatively, you may want to invite guests to bring their own instruments or a favorite record.

CEREMONY. It is customary for the bride and groom to write their own ceremony, reflecting their own tastes suitable to the occasion. *Vern* and *LaVerne* wanted their wedding to be a "rite of passage" from the empty, structured urban life they had known to a new rural life based on community and trusting and showing concern for tradition and love of the land, and they set out to do exactly that. Leaving the Midwestern city in which they had long lived, the couple drove South looking for a community that was just right. A few hours later, they came across a small white frame church in the country. Its oak-shaded yard was crowded with aged parishioners eating fried-chicken lunches and displaying native crafts and abilities. The minister, a kindly old man in a black frock coat and starched shirt, greeted them warmly, and when *Vern* and *LaVerne* indicated their intentions he let out a joyous yell and slapped his thigh. "Bust my buttons! Caroline, fetch my collar!" he whooped and shouted. In no time, the entire congregation was seated in the church and singing old-time shape-note hymns, fanning vigorously, and crying "Amen!" at every opportunity.

Minister: Well, Lord, You sure gave us one heck of a hard winter and I reckon some of us wondered if there'd be no end to it, but, dang it, this troubled ol' earth just keeps a-rotatin' and here we are at plantin' time agin and the trees are puttin' out their blossoms and the ol' bull is lookin' across the fence at the heifers and it sorta speaks to us of what they call *renewal* and *rededication*, don't it?

And that's why we're here today, ain't it, Lord, 'cause these-here kids want ter sorta carry on them *natural processes* and kinder do their part to *create life* and be what Y'might call *at one* with You and each other and the trees and the birds and this great big ball of humanity we got down here and what we might call the *life force*—anyhow, that's the way I see it.

Well, Lord, they're a-waitin' for me, and Caroline here is clearin' her throat somethin' fierce, so I guess I said enough, but—well, You take real good care of 'em now, Y'hear? Goodbye, God. Be talkin' to Y'later.

Vern and *LaVerne* also wrote their own vows. *Rod* and *Mary Elizabeth*, on the other hand, employed the regular vows of their church but added two pages of dialogue from "Love Knows No Night"—a scene in which *Curly* and *Jo-Jo*, pinned by the mudslide, promise to love each other forever if they are rescued soon. Or a couple might wish to speak extemporaneously.

LITERATURE. Readings from Walt Whitman, Thoreau, Dylan Thomas, E. E. Cummings, Frost, the Song of Solomon, and Carl Rogers are popular at weddings today, and, properly chosen, can be every bit as personal and creative as your own poems, essays, songs, or articles. The key, of course, is to make them your own, expressing your own feelings and desires.

Sometimes, selections may be incorporated into the ceremony itself. (Some states have recognized Marlowe's "Come live with me and be my love" as a legally binding contract, but be sure to check with local authorities about this, to avoid misunderstandings later.)

Or you might want to write your own literature and incorporate *that* into the ceremony, as a young couple did not long ago who asked that their names not be used:

Man: And shall we then be husband and wife, and love and trust each other in the spirit of mutual adventure and joy, giving nurture and sustenance the one to the other and yet also preserving the independence and solitude of each,——?

Woman: I— I— don't know what to say... just that I'm...

Man: I'm here. Cleave to me.

Woman: ... so happy. Happy and mixed up and— I don't know. It's like—

Man: Like we were two but now we are two in one?

Woman: Like what Carl Rogers once wrote. "When I love you, I am loving myself, for you are me."

Man: "When you love me, you are loving yourself, for I am you."

Both: "When we love ourselves, we are loving the world, for we are it."

Woman: ——, read that short poem you wrote for us recently.

Man: Oh, I don't know—it's sort of personal.

Woman: Please.

Man: Well, all right:

maybe it will always be that sunday when
we sang to the little bouncing ball dribbled
down the dewy grass-green fairways of our
consciousness landing in hard woods of where
and when   so let us always
and not just the day before tomorrow slice
together the loaf of our caring and hook
the fish of our first flowing self no

*kidding swinging love's clubs between
the hazards of water the traps of sand
in the baggy morning crazy happy
yelling "fore! fore!"*

Woman: ———!
Man: ———!
Or you might enclose your poem in the wedding
invitation or have it printed on napkins. *Stan* and *Debbi*,
although they were not poets, nonetheless wanted their
wedding to be a "marriage of minds" and a time of shar-
ing with family and friends, and sent out the invitations
three months before, including a short reading list:
"Bhagavad Gita"
"Couples," Updike
"Crime and Punishment," Dostoevski
"The Golden Bough," Frazer
"The Great Gatsby," Fitzgerald
"How to Be Your Own Best Friend,"
    Newman & Berkowitz
"On Aggression," Lorenz
"The Portable Nietzsche," Nietzsche
"The Republic," Plato
"Them," Oates
"Zen and the Art of Motorcycle Maintenance," Pirsig
    In the church, the couple entered together from
the rear and sat in front facing the guests. The attendants
passed up and down the aisles distributing notebooks
and pencils. The minister introduced *Stan* and *Debbi*,
who took turns addressing the audience from a small
lectern. *Debbi* spoke on "Views of Home in Post-Marriage
Culture." *Stan* spoke on "The Goddess and the Mom:
Woman as Totemic Figure and Family Technician in
Contemporary Mythology." After a brief discussion and
a multiple-choice quiz, the service was over. (To con-

serve time, *Stan* and *Debbi* had been married three weeks before at their apartment.)

Or you can simply speak to each guest briefly during the reception, to make sure the main points of your wedding are clearly understood. And if you have already selected your married life style you may wish to discuss that, too.

CHARLES McGRATH &
DANIEL MENAKER

Is There No End to PBS Culture?

Reprinted with permission from TV GUIDE ® Magazine.
Copyright © 1975 by Triangle Publications, Inc., Radnor,
Pennsylvania.

[*The following is a glimpse of the new British television
series "The Saga of Culture," soon to be aired on our
own Public Broadcasting System, with an introduction
for American audiences by Joe Garagiola.*]

INTRODUCTION

Joe: Hey there, I'll bet there's a lot of things you don't
know. There were sure a lot of things I didn't know until
I met Sir Arbiter Soup, Kenelm Digby Professor of
Physics and Lapinology at Magdalen College, Oxford,
and a heck of a nice guy. For the next 13 weeks, Sir A

is going to talk to us about what's been going on around here for the last 5000 years. We call it *(cut to titles; Purcell's "Trumpet Voluntary" in background)—The Saga of Culture.*

EPISODE 1
Sir Arbiter (sitting before a fire and stroking a cat; dressed in a blazer, cricket whites and boater): Where did it all begin? How did we get where we are? *(Pauses, takes out pipe, lights it.)* Where do we go from here? *(Fetches decanter, pours sherry, sniffs, sips, drains glass, banks fire and puts out cat.)* Does a flush beat a straight? *(Refill on sherry.)* Not easy questions. One might almost say hard questions—perhaps even stumpers. But if you will share these evenings with me, perhaps together we can stumble upon some answers, or at least pick up a couple of bimbos. *(Another refill; lets cat back in.)* In this first hour we shall be, as it were, skipping hither and yon, establishing the general lines of our inquiry. We call this hour *(strains of "There's No Business Like Show Business" in background)* "The Dogs of Change."

(Dissolve on Sir A, swigging from decanter, and cut to him sitting in a shopping cart in the parking lot of the Food Fair in Yaphank, Long Island.)
    Sir A: Some say that our long climb out of the primordial soup may have begun here *(stretches arms wide; Mantovani can be heard, faintly)* in the Olduvai Gorge... *(Looks around, takes nervous pull from hip flask. Cut to Olduvai Gorge.)* Here in the Olduvai Gorge. Some say that the climb began elsewhere, possibly in Jersey City. Whatever. In any event, five years ago Dr. Louis Leakey unearthed here a pocket comb and the keys to a 1917 Hispano-Suiza. *(Close-up of comb and keys, back-lit.)* From this the chap deduced that Australopithecus may well have been the first to comb his car.

Poppycock! What matters most to the Saga of Culture, don't you see, is the change from the nomadic life to a fixed agrarian society...

(Cut to farm in Somerset, England; Sir A, wearing bib overalls, feeding slops to swine.)
Sir A: I'm here at the farm of Thomas Shandy, which to my mind represents the culmination, the apogee, the peak, if you will—or even if you won't—of English bucolic life. *(Puts down slop bucket, takes long swig from hip flask, saunters over to where Farmer Tom is pitching hay.)* The English yeoman farmer, like all his brethren since the time of the metamorphosis of man the hunter *(Homa venator*, in the Latin) to man the culti-vator *(Homo agricola)*, draws sustenance and wisdom from his native ground *(terra naturalis)*. From the roots, herbs and kohlrabi he gathers...
Farmer Tom *(shouldering Sir A aside and peering into the camera):* Is this for the telly, then? Are you here for the UFOs? Poor Alf, they carried him off last night. All yellow and pink they was, with a tuft of hair growing out the back. I says to the missus, I says, "It's petrol they're after. They use it to make their beer. They suck it up with long hoses, see..." *(Large hook appears camera left, moves horizontally, engages Farmer Tom by the neck, and drags him off.)*
Sir A: Quite. *(Takes nervous pull from flask; weaves uncertainly toward farmhouse, camera right; bends over, snatches up a chicken and tucks it under his arm.)*

(Cut to Jeu de Paume museum, in Paris, and Sir A, wearing beret and artist's smock, standing in front of Manet's "Le Déjeuner sur L'Herbe.")
Sir A: Over the centuries, artists have been fasci-nated with the pastoral ideal. Edouard Manet took this theme and, in this famous painting, transformed it into a nice piece of cheesecake. The very first thing we notice

119

about this masterpiece is that it is vaguely rectangular in shape and, *mirabile dictu!*, suspended from a wall. How convenient, for if it lay upon the floor we should have to crane. Note here the fruitful volumes, the irregular—one might almost say jaunty—disposition of the figures, the dynamic interplay of light and shadow, the volumetric modeling of the pectoral areas. Note, finally, the expression of the woman in the right foreground. Who is this woman who regards us with such bemusement? What does her half smile suggest about the level of dentistry in the late 19th century? What, finally, is she saying to us today? "Will you still respect me in the morning?" Or is her expression as unreadable as the blank enigma that confronts us here...

(Cut to Easter Island and Sir A, wearing Bermuda shorts and flowered sport shirt, standing beside one of the heads. "Also Sprach Zarathustra" thunders in background.)

Sir A (shouting): The meaning of these great stone heads has puzzled generations of archaeologists and telephone repairmen, and theories of their origin are as numerous as wogs in the Punjab. Professor Schliemann, who never saw them at all, held that they were weathercocks. Levi-Strauss has argued that they are early, somewhat oversized examples of dashboard statuary. And Leakey thinks they are all that remain of the South Pacific Professional Bowlers' Hall of Fame. Whatever the case may be, we can say one thing with certainty: they have no arms or legs!

(Cut to blast furnace in a steel mill in Scranton, Pa.; Sir A, wearing helmet and goggles, holding a can of beer. Nearby, a steelworker, stripped to the waist, opens grate and stokes roaring flames.)

Sir A: It was here in the West—though not notably in the indolent Mediterranean areas—that man, through the machine, began to tame his environment. Steel mills like this one provide some of the essential materials for such wonders of technology as the Saturn rocket, the cyclotron, and the Kitchen Magician, which chops, slices, dices, peels, shreds, mashes, hashes and juliennes. And for a limited time only, for $3.59 ($4.59 for stereo tapes) extra, includes an album you cannot buy in any record store—"100 Great Songs of the Korean Conflict Sung by Rosemary Clooney and Vic Damone."

(Cut to Sir A, again sitting before fire in smoking jacket, sipping sherry, stroking cat.)
Sir A: There you have it, then. A preliminary, panoptic look at some of the subjects we shall be investigating in detail over the next twelve Tuesday evenings. *(He rises, sways unsteadily and sits down.)* I hope you can join me here next week for an episode we call *("Trumpet Voluntary" wells in background)* "Problem Dandruff and the Waning of the Middle Ages."

EPILOGUE
Joe: Pretty interesting, huh? If you liked that, you'll want to stay tuned. In just a few minutes Anthony Hopkins will interview Alistair Cooke about why there's always an Oriental-rug backdrop for BBC interviews. In the meantime, this is Pledge Week...

THOMAS MEEHAN

The Word
This Morning
(After One Journey
Too Many Along the
Rialto With THE
NEW YORK TIMES
Drama Staff)

Reprinted by permission of Esquire Magazine, © 1961 by
Esquire, Inc.
Included in the collection YMA, AVA; YMA, ABBA; YMA, OONA;
YMA, IDA; YMA, AGA...AND OTHERS. Copyright © 1959, 1960,
1961, 1962, 1963, 1964, 1965, 1966, 1967 by Thomas Meehan.
Reprinted by permission of Simon & Schuster, Inc.

Sunday, April 5: The word this morning is that Desmond
Leslie, last represented locally two seasons ago by *Call
Me a Taxi,* has put the finishing touches on a new play.
Martinis for Breakfast is the title, and you may put it
down as a contemporary romantic comedy with satiric
overtones. Mr. Leslie, who has lately been dividing his
literary labors between New York and Hollywood, sends
word from his West Coast atelier that the leading roles
are right for Dame Sybil Thorndike and Marlon Brando,
and further advises that the script has been perused by
these luminaries, that interest has been shown, and that

the day of drawing up the contracts is not far distant. Should Dame Sybil and Mr. Brando, then, be willing, and all other arrangements satisfactorily worked out, we may expect the offering in these provinces sometime in late September at a theatre yet to be named. Let it be known, too, that Mr. Leslie will himself produce the offering, in association with Hal Lishness, a California talent agent making his initial entrance into the producing ranks.

Sunday, May 31: A pair of busy gentlemen are Desmond Leslie and Hal Lishness! (For those who came in late, this is the duo who will introduce Mr. Leslie's new play, *Martinis for Breakfast*, here next September.) Their current quest: a director for the romantic comedy. Leading candidates: Peter Glenville and Jean-Louis Barrault. Thus last week a whirlwind four-day trip from Los Angeles to New York to London to Paris and back. Spoke at some length with Mr. Glenville, spoke with M. Barrault. As yet, however, no final decision from either quarter.

P.S. Between planes here, copies of *Martinis for Breakfast* were left with Arlene Francis and Martin Gabel who, advise the Messrs. Leslie and Lishness, are right for the leading roles.

Sunday, June 14: Pencil-in the Music Box as the theatre for the new Desmond Leslie play, *Martinis for Breakfast.* The romantic comedy, which will be presented here under the banner of Leslish Productions, is scheduled to begin rehearsals on October 5, open in New Haven on October 26, move to Boston on November 2, and make its local bow on November 18. Though contracts haven't yet been inked, it's no secret that Katina Paxinou and Chester Morris are being sought for the leads and that the directorial reins will be taken up by Harold Clurman or José Quintero.

Sunday, September 27: Producer-playwright Desmond

Leslie and co-producer Hal Lishness have postponed their production of Mr. Leslie's romantic comedy, *Martinis for Breakfast.* They await the availability of an actress (identity a deep, dark secret as of this morning's bulletin) currently committed to a movie. Look, then, to late October for rehearsals and an early December première in New York at a theatre still to be determined. It may incidentally further be disclosed that the producers are negotiating with George Abbott to direct the entry.

Sunday, November 8: Now it can be told! The actress for whom Desmond Leslie and Hal Lishness have been delaying their contemplated production of *Martinis for Breakfast* is Janet Murray. Seems the well known motion-picture star has been longing to return to the New York stage. She read the script several months ago, wanted very much to play the lead, but, alas, picture commitments stood in the way. All that is now ancient history, however. The picture commitments have been filled, terms agreed upon, and for the Messrs. Leslie and Lishness it's full speed ahead. Advises Mr. Leslie: look for an early January opening at a theatre yet to be chosen.

P.S. A check of the archives reveals that Miss Murray has been absent from the Broadway stage since 1936, when she appeared here in *Alive and Kicking.*

Sunday, November 29: From the Sitting-on-the-Fence Department: He hasn't said "yes," he hasn't said "no"—he being Sir Ralph Richardson, the subject at hand being the lead opposite Janet Murray in Desmond Leslie's new play, *Martinis for Breakfast.* The messenger carrying this tale of Hamlet-like indecision: Hal Lishness, co-producer with Mr. Leslie of the January offering. Having just returned from a trip to the West End and a long huddle with Sir Ralph, Mr. Lishness hints that the answer will be an emphatic "yes," and that contracts will be signed in London before the week is out. At the moment, however, official acceptance by the English actor is still awaited.

Sunday, December 20: Thorne Peters has been signed to play opposite Janet Murray in the forthcoming *Martinis for Breakfast.* The appearance will mark the young actor's Broadway debut, although, it may be noted, he is no stranger to the legitimate stage, having played several seasons at the Pasadena Playhouse in addition to his many television roles.

Sunday, January 17: Pencil-in the Henry Miller as the theatre for the new Desmond Leslie play, *Martinis for Breakfast.* The romantic comedy, with a cast headed by Janet Murray and Thorne Peters, will be placed in rehearsal on February 8, open in Wilmington on February 23, move to Philadelphia on March 2, and make its local bow on March 16. Mike Nichols is being sought to direct the entry.

Sunday, January 31: Mark yet another director making the move up from the ranks of television to Broadway. He is Dan Thrasher, and he has been commissioned by Leslish Productions to stage *Martinis for Breakfast*, the Desmond Leslie comedy which will star Janet Murray and Thorne Peters. Mr. Thrasher, by the way, does not come to his Broadway assignment completely without theatrical experience. He was the director two years ago of a summer touring company of *Springtime for Henry.*

Wednesday, February 3: Amanda Dee Jones, Henry Haversham, Walter Docker, and Linda Dowling have been signed to roles in *Martinis for Breakfast,* the Desmond Leslie comedy scheduled to arrive at the Henry Miller on March 16.

Monday, February 8: Rehearsals begin today for *Martinis for Breakfast,* the Desmond Leslie play featuring Janet Murray and Thorne Peters which will première here on March 16.

Thursday, February 25: By the time Desmond Leslie's *Martinis for Breakfast* arrives at the Henry Miller on March 16 it may easily have established a record as the most rewritten play of the season. Hal Lishness, co-producer of the work with Mr. Leslie, advised yesterday in Wilmington, where the romantic comedy opened on Tuesday evening to generally unfavorable notices, that a new third act was put in last night and that a new second act will be inserted for this evening's performance. The revisions, Mr. Lishness explained, will make the play both "more Shavian and artistically more sound." The work, which is being directed by Dan Thrasher, stars Janet Murray and Thorne Peters.

Saturday, February 27: Dan Thrasher has withdrawn as director of *Martinis for Breakfast,* the Desmond Leslie comedy now on its pre-Broadway tour in Wilmington. "There were certain basic differences in aesthetic interpretation between myself and the playwright which could not honestly be compromised," Mr. Thrasher stated. "The parting was perfectly amicable," the director added. A spokesman for the play announced last night that Mr. Leslie himself would replace Mr. Thrasher at the directorial helm.

Thursday, March 4: Further overhauling caused the cancellation of last night's performance, at the Shubert Theatre in Philadelphia, of Desmond Leslie's *Martinis for Breakfast.* A spokesman for Leslish Productions, under whose banner the offering will be introduced here on March 16, advised yesterday in Philadelphia, where the romantic comedy opened on Tuesday evening to generally unfavorable notices, that Mr. Leslie has drafted a new first act which will be put into the play tomorrow night, when the work will resume its pre-Broadway run.

Tuesday, March 9: Ill-health has caused Janet Murray to withdraw from a major role in Desmond Leslie's *Martinis for Breakfast*, currently trying out in Philadelphia. "The recurrence of an old back injury sustained some years ago while working in a Boston Blackie movie has reluctantly forced me to give up the role," Miss Murray explained yesterday, before leaving for her home in Los Angeles. "The withdrawal was perfectly amicable on both sides, and I wish the entire cast all the best," the actress added, refusing to comment on a rumored rift between herself and Mr. Leslie. No replacement has been engaged as yet, a spokesman for the play announced last night. It is reported that the producers are seeking Katharine Cornell for the role.

Thursday, March 11: Joanne Millwood has stepped into the part relinquished earlier this week by Janet Murray in Desmond Leslie's *Martinis for Breakfast*. The comedy, which is in its pre-Broadway run in Philadelphia, is scheduled to arrive at the Henry Miller on March 16. The appearance will mark the New York debut for Miss Millwood, a television actress who in private life is Mrs. Hal Lishness.

Saturday, March 13: The opening of *Martinis for Breakfast* has been set back two weeks from March 16 to March 30. Reason: more time needed for new revisions and for Joanne Millwood, who earlier this week replaced Janet Murray in a major role, to work into the part. The play will extend its pre-Broadway run at the Shubert Theatre in Philadelphia for another two weeks.

Thursday, March 25: The rumor that *Martinis for Break-*

fast, the Desmond Leslie comedy currently trying out in Philadelphia, would close out-of-town without coming to New York was emphatically denied yesterday by the playwright. "We will definitely open as scheduled," Mr. Leslie stated in a telephone interview from Philadelphia.

Tuesday, March 30: Opening Tonight: *Martinis for Breakfast,* a new comedy by Desmond Leslie, produced by Leslish Productions, staged by the playwright, and starring Thorne Peters and Joanne Millwood, with Amanda Dee Jones, Henry Haversham, Walter Docker, and Linda Dowling. At Henry Miller's Theatre, 124 West 43rd Street, at 8 o'clock sharp.

Sunday, April 4: Scoreboard: *Martinis for Breakfast*— Desmond Leslie's new play—failed to please any of the aisle-sitters. Said the *News:* "Very little kick in Mr. Leslie's Martinis." Added the *Post:* "Old-fashioned as it may sound, I'll stick to orange juice for my matutinal repast." Our man gives *his* reasons why not in the usual place on the left.

Monday, April 5: Closed Saturday night, after seven performances: *Martinis for Breakfast.*

Two years later, Sunday, April 16: The word this morning is that Desmond Leslie, last represented locally two seasons ago by *Martinis for Breakfast,* has put the finishing touches on a new play. *Does She or Doesn't She?* is the title, and you may put it down as a contemporary romantic...

Yma Dream

Reprinted by permission; © 1962 The New Yorker
Magazine, Inc.
Included in the collection YMA, AVA; YMA, ABBA; YMA, OONA;
YMA, IDA; YMA, AGA...AND OTHERS. Copyright © 1959, 1960,
1961, 1962, 1963, 1964, 1965, 1966, 1967 by Thomas Meehan.
Reprinted by permission of Simon & Schuster, Inc.

In this dream, which I have had on the night of the full
moon for the past three months, I am giving a cocktail
party in honor of Yma Sumac, the Peruvian singer. This
is strange at once, for while I have unbounded admiration
for four-octave voices, I have never met Miss Sumac,
and, even in a dream, it seems unlikely that I should be
giving her a party. No matter. She and I are in the small
living room of my apartment, on Charles Street, in
Greenwich Village, and we are getting along famously. I
have told her several of my Swedish-dialect stories, and
she has reciprocated by singing for me, in Quechua, a

medley of Andean folk songs. Other guests are expected momentarily. I have no idea, however, who any of them will be. Miss Sumac is wearing a blue ball gown and I am in white tie and tails. Obviously, despite the somewhat unfashionable neighborhood and the cramped quarters of my apartment, it is to be a pretty swell affair. In any case, I have spread several dishes of Fritos about the room, and on what is normally my typing table there is a bowl of hot *glügg*.

The doorbell rings. A guest! I go to the door, and there, to my astonished delight, is Ava Gardner. This is going to be a bit of all right, I think.

"Tom, darling!" she says, embracing me warmly. "How wonderful of you to have asked me."

In my waking hours, unfortunately, I have never met Miss Gardner. In my dream, though, my guests seem to know me rather intimately, while, oddly, none of them seem to know each other. Apparently it is their strong common affection for me that has brought them to Charles Street. For my part, although I immediately recognize each guest as he or she arrives, I have no memory of having ever met any of them, or, for that matter, of having invited them to a party in my apartment. On with the dream, however. "Miss Ava Gardner," I say, "I'd like you to meet Miss Yma Sumac."

"Charmed," says Miss Sumac.

"Delighted," counters Miss Gardner.

"Ah, but Tom," says Miss Sumac, with an enchanting laugh (which runs up the scale from E above middle C to C above high C), "let us not, on this of all occasions, be formal. *Por favor*, introduce each guest only by the first name, so that we may all quickly become—how shall I say?—*amigos*."

Typical Peruvian friendliness, I think, and reintroduce the two. "Ava, Yma," I say.

We sit around for some time, sipping *glügg* and munching Fritos. Things seem to be going well. The doorbell rings again. The second guest is a man—Abba Eban, the former Israeli Ambassador to the United Nations. Again I make the introductions, and, bowing to the wishes of the guest of honor, keep things on a first-name basis. "Abba, Yma; Abba, Ava," I say.

I stifle a grin, but neither Miss Sumac nor my two other guests see anything amusing in the exchange. We chat. The bells rings again, and I am pleased to find Oona O'Neill, Charlie Chaplin's wife, at the door. She is alone. I bring her into the room. "Oona, Yma; Oona, Ava; Oona, Abba," I say.

We are standing in a circle now, smiling brightly but not talking much. I sense a slight strain, but the party is young and may yet come to life. The bell again. It is another man—Ugo Betti, the Italian playwright. A bit hurriedly, I introduce him to the circle. "Ugo, Yma; Ugo, Ava; Ugo, Oona; Ugo, Abba," I say.

Miss Sumac gives me an enigmatic glance that I try to interpret. Boredom? Thirst? No, she looks almost *irritated.* Hastily, I replenish everyone's glass. For some reason, I begin to hope that no other guests have been invited. The doorbell rings once again, however, and I open the door on two lovely actresses, Ona Munson and Ida Lupino. This gives me a happy inspiration for my introductions. "Ona and Ida," I say, "surely you know Yma and Ava? Ida, Ona—Oona, Abba." Damn! It doesn't come out even. "Ida, Ona—Ugo," I finish lamely.

I have scarcely given Miss Munson and Miss Lupino their first drinks when I am again summoned to the door. My guests stand stony-faced as I usher in the new arrival, the young Aga Khan. He is looking exceptionally well turned out in a dinner jacket with a plaid cummerbund. Smiling too cheerfully, I introduce him to the waiting group. "Folks," I say, using a word I have always detested, "here's the Aga Khan! *You* know." But there is silence, so I must continue. "Aga—Yma, Ava, Oona, Ona 'n' Ida, Abba 'n' Ugo."

The Aga Khan and Mr. Eban, I notice, take an immediate dislike to each other, and I begin to feel an unmistakable pall descending over my party. I suggest a game of charades. This is met with glacial looks from everyone, including Miss Gardner, whose earlier affection for me has now totally vanished. When the doorbell rings this time, everybody turns and glares at the door. I open it and discover another pair—Ira Wolfert, the novelist, and Ilya Ehrenburg, the *Russian* novelist. The latter, I know, is quite a man-of-the-world, so I try a new approach. "Ilya," I say, "why don't you just introduce yourself and Ira? You know all these lovely people, don't you?"

"*Nyet,*" says Mr. Ehrenburg. "Can't say that I do."

"Oh, all *right,*" I say. "Ilya, Ira, here's Yma, Ava, Oona. Ilya, Ira—Ona, Ida, Abba, Ugo, Aga."

I ask Miss Sumac to sing for us. She refuses. We continue with the *glügg* and some hopelessly inane small talk. Mr. Eban and the Aga Khan stand at opposite sides of the room, eying each other. I begin to wish I'd never given the goddam party. Ona Munson jostles Ugo Betti's elbow by accident, spilling his drink. I spring forward to put them at their ease, whipping a handkerchief from my pocket. "Never mind!" I cry. "No damage done! Ugo, you go get yourself another drink. I'll just wipe this *glügg* off the, uh, *rügg.*" The guests fix me with narrowed eyes. At this moment, Eva Gabor, the Hungarian actress, sweeps through the door, which I have cleverly left open. Unaware of the way things are going, she embraces me and turns, beaming, to meet the others. Inevitably, I must make the introductions. I start rapidly. "Eva, meet Yma and Ava and Oona—" But then I find that Miss Gabor is pausing to hug each guest in turn, so I am forced to make the remaining introductions separately. "Eva, Ona; Eva, Ida; Eva, Ugo; Eva, Abba; Eva, Ilya; Eva, Ira; Eva, Aga."

This is a *terrible* party. All the men have bunched up. We stand in a circle, glowering at one another. I can think of nothing to say. I feel oddly hemmed in, like a man who is about to be stoned to death.

"Am I late?" asks the actress Uta Hagen gaily as she comes tripping into the room.

"No, no!" I say, gallantly taking her arm and steering her at once toward the punch bowl and away from the others.

"Please have the common decency to introduce your guests to one another," says Miss Sumac, in a cold monotone. "And in the proper manner."

In the dream, Yma Sumac seems to have some kind of hold over me, and I must do as she wishes. "O.K., O.K.," I snap crossly. "Uta, Yma; Uta, Ava; Uta, Oona; Uta, Ona; Uta, Ida; Uta, Ugo; Uta, Abba; Uta, Ilya; Uta, Ira; Uta, Aga; Uta, Eva." I turn to see if this has placated Miss Sumac, but she coldly ignores me. I have begun to hate her. Then I discover that the *glügg* has run out, and I am forced to offer my guests rye-and-7-Up. In the hope that no further company will arrive, I silently close the door. The bell rings instantly, however, and I feel a chill run down my spine. I pretend not to hear it.

"Answer the door," Miss Sumac says peremptorily. My circle of guests moves menacingly toward me. With a plummeting heart, I open the door. Standing before me, in immaculate evening dress, is a sturdy, distinguished-looking man. He is the Polish concert pianist Mieczyslaw Horszowski.

"Come in, Mieczyslaw!" I cry, with tears in my eyes. "I've never been so glad to see anyone in my whole life!"

And here, always, my dream ends.

MICHAEL O'DONOGHUE

Pornocopia

First published in the *National Lampoon*. © 1970 Michael O'Donoghue. Reprinted by permission of Michael O'Donoghue.

THE ELEGANT ENGLISH EPISTOLARY EROTICISM
Mr. N... chanc'd to offer a bout of dalliance and disport. My blush serv'd but to inflame the young gentleman's ardours, and a heart-fetch'd sigh at the size of his re- markable fouling piece banish'd all reserve. Canting up my petticoats and unlacing my stays, I fell supine on the settee, my exquisite treasures at his disposal. Thus embolden'd, he took in hand the prodigious engine and, abandoning restraint, remm'd the rubid cleft where grows the wanton moss that crowns the brow of modesty, but to naught avail. Thrice again the frightful machine

MICHAEL O'DONOGHUE

assail'd the region of delight which, with maidenhead's sweet mant'ling, celebrates the triumph of roses o'er the lily, but that delicious cloven spot, the fairest mark for his well-mettl'd member, quell'd and abash'd the gallant intruder. Mustering his fervour, once more didst Cupid's capt'n 'tempt to brunt the fierce prow of his formidable vessel past the shoals of luxuriant umberage which garland'd my rutt'd charms and into that uncloy'd cove where humid embars blaz'd on visitation, yet was, e'en so, repulst. Tho' toss'd 'twixt profusion and compliance, my hand crept softly to the sturdy lad's ripen'd tussle and roam'd the sprout'd tufts, whilst he my hillocks wander'd, then rekindl'd his nobly stock'd conduits, distend'd the proud steed, where'pon I near swoon'd of extasy's bright tumult as the sturdy stallion, his exhaultations fir'd, gallop'd o'er ev'ry hedge and thicket, spending the jetty sprig, won the sally, and gain'd a lodgement. Encircl'd in the pleasure-girst, ingorg'd by dissolution's tender agony, each 'fusive stroke stirr'd my in'most tendrils, devolv'd my dewy furrow of its secrets, which I, flush with straddl'd frolik, was far from disrelishing, 'til, somewhat appeas'd, his quiv'ling extremity, twin'd by unquench'd appetite, durst 'frock the fury of unflagg'd inspersions, yet homeward play'd my rake the plenteous protraction, redoubl'd his endeavours that joy's thrust might soon drink deep at rapture's well, then didst, at last, sheath, to the churl'd hilt, his massy weapon, and so suffer'd me to bliss.

> I am
>> Madam,
>>> Yours, etc., etc., etc.

THE FIN-DE-SIÈCLE BRITISH BIRCHING BOOK

"And what might your name be, my child?" inquired Lord Randy Stoker, removing a tin of violet pastilles from the pocket of his tangerine-velvet waistcoat and placing one in his sensuous mouth while his flashing eyes coolly probed the buxom lass that sat trembling before him.

"My name's Miss Prissy Trapp, sir." she replied in a faint voice and working-class accent, lowered her eyes, and curtsied. "I'm the new maid."

"Welcome to Felonwart, my remote country manor house. I can assure you that your stay here will be most ... amusing. Come into the drawing room and place yourself at the disposal of my guests."

The drawing room was that of a typical country manor house, save for the fact that the walls were padded, the windows barred, a curious array of whips and riding equipage was displayed above the fireplace, an immodest fresco graced the north wall, a number of cages hung suspended from the ceiling and, in the center of the room, towering above a bloodstained altar, loomed a moonstone-studded effigy of Kā, the nineteen-armed Babylonian Goddess of Lust.

"As you may have gathered, my tastes run some-what toward the *outré*," Lord Stoker commented, helping himself to another violet pastille, and continued, his voice dark with menace, "a proclivity that does not limit itself to décor."

Upon seeing Prissy, a tall, gaunt man, wearing but a pair of soiled galoshes, threw himself at her feet and commenced wildly kissing her feather duster.

"Allow me to introduce Professor Schadenfreude," interposed Lord Stoker as the bewildered miss blushed crimson under the Austrian's singular attention. "His studies in aberrant behavior have taken man's sexual urges out of the Dark Ages."

"And back to the Stone Age," added Lady Wick-Burner, crawling across the carpet to gnaw on the heel of Prissy's left shoe.

"Oh... Oh... Please... I beseech you... Leave off ... Have pity... Oh... No more...," pleaded the misused maid.

Delighted by the young girl's supplications, the Duke of Pudenda discontinued reading from a slim volume of unseemly sonnets he had recently published privately in a limited edition of four copies, all of which were bound in tinted wildebeest.

MICHAEL O'DONOGHUE

"Remove her chemise!" demanded Reverend John Thomas.

Upon hearing this, Prissy, her face a mask of abasement, attempted to flee but was thwarted by two Nubian eunuchs who, despite the unfortunate's pathetic struggles, firmly secured her wrists with braided peacock tails.

"All in good time," cautioned the Sultana of Zosh. "First, allow the hapless servant to gaze upon the instrument of her chastisement." She drew back the drapes to reveal a weird machine composed of a steam engine, pistons, manacles, a glass godemiche, rubber tubing, a gilded harpsichord, a whalebone corset, asparagus tips and a vat of scented lard.

The Sultana smiled wanly and murmured, "We call it... 'The Blind Chicken!'"

"What does it do?" asked Prissy.

Silhouetted against the dying sunlight, the great circle of Kā's nineteen arms appeared to be a ceaseless juggernaut of shame and degradation as Lord Stoker leaned over to whisper. "You'll discover that only too soon," and stuck his purple tongue in her ear.

THE EARLY FRENCH ALGOLAGNIC NOVEL
The Comte was in the formal gardens whipping his linoleum when he was joined by the Bishop. Ceasing his exertions, he greeted the prelate, and said:

"You are undoubtedly curious why I am whipping my linoleum. And yet, on closer examination, nothing could be more natural... or might I say 'unnatural,' as they are the same thing. Man, it goes without saying, is intrinsically evil, bearing in mind, of course, that good and evil, vice and virtue, exist only within the confines of society. It is the laws which cause crime, for, without law, there is no crime. Nature capriciously destroys the fools who forsake their instinctual lust and hunger in the name of virtue, as Nature does us all. Man is an animal with a soul that exists only through sensations. Although man must not limit his actions, there is no free will, therefore he is not responsible for his actions. Quite obviously, the more disgusting the act, the greater the pleasure, and since pleasure, or might I say 'pain,' as pleasure is but pain diminished, remains the chief aim of all human existence, it should be enjoyed at any cost, particularly at the expense of other people, that is to say, not only is there joy in whipping my linoleum, but there is also joy in reflecting upon those who are not allowed to whip their linoleum. Hence, cruelty is nothing more than man's life force uncorrupted by civilization. As we are pawns to misery, so must we dispense misery to pawns. Since pain is the absolute, it is essential that I, as a philosopher, pursue this absolute. So it seems that the question, my dear Bishop, is not 'Why do I whip my linoleum?' but rather, 'Why doesn't everyone whip his linoleum?'"

THE RECENT FRENCH ALGOLAGNIC NOVEL*
The moon was partially obscured by a cloud.

One afternoon, a limousine had picked up E at the Buttes-Chaumont Gardens, the Bois de Vincennes, the Bassin de la Villette, or perhaps the Boulevard Haussmann, and had taken her to a *château* in southern France. The driver had departed without saying a word.

Attendants prepared E for the party that evening. She was dressed in a bird costume resembling a boat-tailed grackle. I am certain that she was forbidden to speak.

In another version, the limousine picks up E at the Bureau des Objets Trouvés.

E was placed on the lawn and instructed to remain there until summoned. Behind her was a row of cypress trees. Under the third tree lay a pale blue envelope. From

*Ed. Note—Rumored to be the work of A.... M....., noted Marxist author and art critic.

the envelope she withdrew a photograph of three persons on an ottoman. One is blindfolded. It is difficult to determine what they are engaged in.

Her costume was perfect in every detail. The only discrepancy that might prompt the casual observer to conclude that E could be something other than an enormous boat-tailed grackle was a pair of black patent leather shoes which she is required to wear as a symbol of her absolute subjugation.

Although forbidden to speak, I believe that E was allowed to whistle.

The bird costume restricted movement and it often took E over an hour to reach places only a few feet away.

When she glances back to the third tree, she notices that the pale blue envelope and the photograph are missing.

That evening, three men, X. Y, and Z, retire from the party to chat beneath the porte-cochere. Y is her lover.

Fragments of conversation are audible from where E is standing on the lawn.

"Have you spoken to G lately?"

"It's odd you should ask. Why only last week..."

The three men turn toward her. X and Z appear familiar, as if she had seen them in a photograph.

"Look, there's a boat-tailed grackle," remarks Z. "An uncommonly large one, I might add."

Moments pass. The men do not move. E observes the moon clearly reflected in her black patent leather shoes. Surely her lover will recognize her, take her in his arms, and debase her in the fashion which she has grown to regard so dearly. She flaps her wings and whistles frantically.

Finally, Y speaks.

"One seldom sees them so far north this late in the season."

EXPURGATION BY LATIN

Now there once lived near Genoa a wealthy merchant named Gelfardo, who was infatuated with Bonella, a miller's daughter unsurpassed in beauty, grace, and charm.

As it happened, Bonella, spurning Gelfardo's advances, was wont to seek diversion with a certain abbot, but he, much to her displeasure, had given to *concilium loqui* swans.

One afternoon, while strolling in the forest, Gelfardo came upon the comely damsel picking flowers. With a lascivious wink, he asked the lady if she might care to unfasten her bodice and *supplicia eorum, qui in furto aut latrocinio aut aliqua noxia sint comprehensi gratiora dis immortalibus esse arbitrantur* for an hour or so.

She coyly agreed to the merchant's bold overtures, but on two conditions. The first was that he pay her 200 gold ducats; the second, that after he had *supplicia eorum qui in furto aut latrocinio aut aliqua noxia sint comprehensi gratiora dis immortalibus esse arbitrantur,* then she, in turn could *sed cum eius generis copia defecit etiam ad innocentium supplicia descendunt.*

Suspecting nothing, Gelfardo agreed, gave her 200 gold ducats, and made ready to *tantis excitati praemiis et sua sponte multi in disciplinam conveniunt.*

As the couple began *haec poena apud eos est gravissima,* who should pass by but the abbot. Upon seeing the *consuerunt neque tributa,* he took three potatoes and a long loaf of bread from his sack and *quibus ita est interdictum, hi numero impiorum ac sceleratorum habentur his omnes decedunt, aditum eorum sermonemque defugiunt,* which he then tied to Bonella's *honos ullus communicatur.*

Waiting until the merchant had almost *hoc proprium virtutis existimant,* the abbot sprang from behind the bushes where he had been hiding and shouted, *"Expulsos agris finitimos cedere!"* Startled, Bonella *neque quemquam prope audere consistere; simul hoc se fore tutiores arbitrantur, repentinae incursionis timore sublato,* causing the string to *suumque auxilium* Gelfardo's *pollicentur atque a multitudine collaudantur* and *qui ex his secuti non sunt, in desertorum ac proditorum numero decuntur, omniumque his rerum postea fides derogatur* the three potatoes.

It was only then that she reminded him of the second condition.

Moral: Cuckolds often make merry but it is rare indeed that *omni Gallia eurum hominum qui aliquo sunt numero atque honore genera sunt duo; nam plebes paene servorum habetur loco, quae nihil audet per se, nulli adhibetur consilio.*

EXPURGATION BY ASTERISKS (CIRCA 1925)

"So this is Paris," mused Lt. Rick Stafford as he climbed the winding stairs that led to the garret of Nana Bijou, the torch singer whose address a doughboy had given him at the front with the words, "Tell her you're a friend of Bob's." He died two days later in a mustard gas attack at Aubers Ridge. Rick had written the letter to his parents. It was difficult to know what to say.

Rick knocked on the door. A woman answered who would have been young if not for her eyes.

"Hello," he said awkwardly. "I'm... a friend of Bob's."

"Bob?" She shook her head. "I don't remember zee names, lieutenant. But I can never forget zee faces, terrible haunted faces zat are stalked by Death. Come in, *mon cher,* and have a glass of absinthe."

The room was small. Faded theatrical posters covered the walls. In the corner stood a *lit à deux places.*

"Have you killed many Boches?" she asked.

"No. I'm an ambulance driver."

He began to talk. The words spilled out. He told

her about his childhood, about his dream of returning to the States and becoming an architect, about the war.

Finally, there was nothing more to say. He stared out the window that overlooked the rooftops of St.-Germain. It had begun to snow. The pigeons had already made tracks around the chimneys.

He turned to her and asked, "Where do you work?"

"In a cheap *café.*" She smiled. "What does zat, or anything else, matter?"

He took her in his arms and kissed her gently. "Nothing matters," he replied, "but we must keep up appearances." He began to unbutton her blouse.
****
****
****
****
****

Afterwards, they smoked cigarettes.

THE BEST SELLER

Lean, tan, blue-eyed Noel Walgreen, idol of millions, sank back into the satin sheets of his round, lavish bed, stared up at the mirrored ceiling that featured his flawless body, and mused over the stunning women he had enjoyed during the last month. He could never forget:

Tracy—By the time she got her name up in lights, they spelled it S-L-U-T!

Lynn—The stormy starlet whose biggest picture was shot with a Polaroid camera!

Mara—Her husband found romance in the arms of another woman... and so did she!

Naomi—The only good impression she made on Hollywood was in Grauman's wet cement!

Ellen—Star of stage, screen, and psycho ward!

Adele—The gossip columnist who could hold the front page... but not the man she loved!

Suzan—Even the Greeks didn't have a word for what she was!

145

MICHAEL O'DONOGHUE

Vicky—She lived every day as though it was the last... and every night as though it was the first!

Melanie—The sex kitten who turned into a hellcat!

Dawn—The hoofer who would one-step her way into a guy's heart... and two-time her way out!

Irene—Her movies got good reviews from everyone but the vice squad!

Nicole—When her agent promised to make her the "toast of the town," she didn't know the town was Tijuana!

Joan—The sultry songstress who knew every 4-letter word... except "love"!

Louise—Fans could find her autograph in any motel register!

Consuelo—The Latin bombshell who went off... with another guy!

Pam—The kind of girl men put on a pedestal just so they can look up her dress!

And, of course, Wendy, his wife, raven-tressed film goddess whose icy beauty had made her the "Queen of Tinseltown." Ten years ago, when he was just a kid back from Korea, he had met her, when she was just a waitress slinging hash at a truck stop in Elbow River, Montana. They were married two days later. Those first years had been happy ones. But that was before they had become stars. Somehow... somewhere... something had been lost in that heady climb to the top. They had become puppets, mere pawns manipulated by shadowy, faceless magnates to further cartels of illusion, caught up in a savage web of greed, lust, and power. Eyes that once sparkled with joy now reflected only the tawdry glitter of flickering limelight. Their souls had drowned in kidney-shaped swimming pools.

The bedroom door swung open and Wendy walked in, nude, her ripe, full breasts glistening with cocoa butter. She was smoking marijuana, or "gage," as the hopheads called it.

146

"I can't go on like this any longer, Wendy, watching you destroy yourself," he said.

"No man in the world is ever going to hurt me again. Not even you, Noel," she commented.

"I made the mistake of thinking we felt the same about each other," he observed.

"You're playing with dynamite! It just may blow up in your face!" she exclaimed.

"Do you know what you want?" he inquired.

"I did once," she answered.

"How could I have been so blind," he concluded and pulled her down onto the bed. His hungry lips sought hers. Together, they scaled the peaks of ecstasy.

When it was over, he caressed her face gently with his hands and whispered, "I love you."

Moments passed. The only sound was the haunting tinkle of their twelve-tiered chandelier. Then she swallowed a handful of amphetamines, or "goof-balls," as the jet-set calls them, paused, and replied, "That and a dime will buy you a cup of coffee."

MARK SINGER

101 Great Government-Toppling Gags

By permission of Mark Singer. © 1977 Mark Singer.

The C.I.A. plotted in 1960 to assassinate Premier Castro with poisoned cigars, Time magazine said yesterday. The C.I.A.'s medical experts concocted a box of "suitably doctored" Havana cigars, but they were never used, the article said, because other C.I.A. employes pointed out that there was no way to assure Premier Castro would not distribute the cigars to other people.
—The New York Times

So, a bunch of wet blankets down at The Company apparently put the kibosh on the old "loaded-cigar" rou-

149

tine, depriving Fidel of the surprise of his life. There are, regrettably, spoilsports like that in every crowd. Fortunately, saner heads have prevailed at the C.I.A. in other instances. Evidence has surfaced recently of an eyes-only file entitled "101 Great Government-Toppling Gags," a rib-tickling primer on some of the hilarious cloak-and-dagger high jinks that the intelligence community has devised to keep the Free World in stitches. Excerpts follow:

The Joy Buzzer. A bit of fiddling with the internal mechanism of your standard hand-held joy buzzer—replacing the penlight battery with a tiny nuclear power cell—can convert this innocent "toy" into a deadly, high-voltage tool of the secret war. Like any device for lethal horseplay, its uses should be restricted, specifically to clandestine assignations with suspected double agents. The following technique is recommended: Meet the double agent in a secluded spot—say, a clearing in a Central American jungle. Carry on a normal conversation, drawing out the expected intelligence data. If the subject seems evasive or insincere, simply pop the straightforward question, "Are you a double agent?" Then, if the double agent appears frightened, reassure him with a warm smile and kind words—something like "April fools!" or "Just joking there, fella" should suffice—and simultaneously offer him a friendly handshake, applying the joy buzzer. The result should be instantaneous. Quickly walk away. A point of caution: immediately return the joy buzzer to its lead-lined safety pouch! Your fellow agents back at headquarters will certainly want to shake your hand when they congratulate you on a mission well done.

The Fly-in-the-Ice-Cube. Not a plastic ice cube and not a plastic fly, but the *genuine articles!* Carry this one in its miniature, pocket-sized, refrigerated carrying case and drop it in your intended victim's drinking glass when he's not looking. If he spots the gag, try to justify it as a harmless bit of boyish self-indulgence. It will boost your credibility if you have replaced the victim's normal drinking glass with a trick "dribble glass," almost always good for a hearty guffaw or two. If your adversary is *not* amused, you'll have to do some fast thinking, perhaps on the order of feigning sudden gastric discomfort. Meanwhile, that "phony" ice cube will be melting, with the "liquidation" (ha! ha!) of the enemy drawing near. Inside that real-life ice cube is, of course, a real-life deadly insect in suspended animation. The killer-bee model has proved highly efficient, and a tsetse-fly option is also available for agents working in appropriate climates.

Rubber Snakes and Spiders. The rubber-snake gimmick is most effective when dealing with a captured enemy agent who is unwilling to "spill the beans." The trick here depends upon a slow but deliberate progression toward the desired end—hard intelligence. A good tactic would be for two agents to work together as a "tough-guy/nice-guy" team. After leaving the subject locked in a small soundproof cell for several days, the "tough guy" should enter the cell and, in a menacing manner, make clear the inevitable consequences of the enemy agent's failure to cooperate. If, after several hours of effort, this attempt at suasion fails, the "tough guy" should be replaced by the "nice guy." It is the "nice guy's" job to offer the enemy agent soothing words, as well as, perhaps, a stick of chewing gum. (For the "nice-guy" ploy to be effective, it is important that he *not* give the enemy either the larky but ineffectual pepper-flavored stick of gum or the kind that catches one's finger in a mousetrap device.) If an extended series of "tough-guy/nice-guy" exchanges fails to elicit the desired information, it would be advisable to begin placing rubber snakes and spiders on the subject's pillow as he sleeps. Upon awaking, he should be willing to talk. If he remains intransigent, the "tough-guy/nice-guy" scenario should be abandoned in favor of one involving real snakes and spiders.

The Squirting Flower. This valuable tool of the espionage trade has often proved its mettle at border crossings, those ticklish exchange points for agents slipping back into the "warm." Under normal working conditions, your fake passport and forged visa should be in good order. But suppose that a suspicious border guard in, for example, Czechoslovakia, smells a rat and decides to detain you. At this point, it is wise to appear to surrender, acknowledging, "O.K., you got me. I'm a spy and there's a tiny transmitter hidden in my boutonniere." When the guard draws near to inspect the flower, you're free to squirt him with your favorite incapacitating substance and then escape, preferably on skis. Always be careful to choose the correct squirting flower for the desired task. The carnation will accommodate a fatal payload of liquid cyanide, but for small-scale jobs—those requiring merely a disabling dosage of Mace—a Veterans of Foreign Wars poppy should do the trick.

The Disappearing-Ink Pen. Long a standby of the diplomatic treaty-signing fraternity, disappearing ink will prove very handy if you are captured by the enemy and forced to sign a trumped-up confession. Other covert uses seem plausible. Suppose, for instance, that you are a secret agent operating undercover abroad as a member of an embassy staff. Suppose further that, while attending a diplomatic dinner, a signal over the surgically-implanted receiver inside your ear informs you that the troublesome world leader seated to your right plans to expose you between the soup and fish courses. Your mission is survival! Waste little time before seizing the chance to show your adversary your disappearing-ink fountain pen. Boldly tell him that it contains disappearing ink, and that you only brought it along to relieve the tedium that inevitably seems to infect state dinners.

Then, with mock clumsiness, spray your adversary with disappearing ink. If he does not immediately disappear, he will certainly leap to his feet with indignation. While mumbling your apology, secretly place an inflated whoopee cushion on his chair. When he retakes his seat, the whoopee cushion should cause him intense embarrassment, unless he is a Balkan. If he is a Balkan, hit him with a faceful of sneezing powder. Then, quickly put on a pair of Groucho Marx glasses, with fake nose and moustache, and quietly slip into the night.

Niles Nitkin Says, "You Can Be a Total Person"

By permission of Mark Singer. © 1977 Mark Singer.

Your typical American "person" begins each day with every good intention, but how often do things flow according to the desired game plan? Another way of asking this question is, "Do you *have* a game plan?" If not, the promise of becoming a Total Person is almost certainly eluding you. It needn't be that way, of course, which is precisely where the *Niles Nitkin Total Person Program* fits in.

THE "SMITHS"
Consider the case of Felix and Bebe "Smith." Two summers ago, while their sons, Todd and Howie, were away at camp learning shrub identification and lathe maintenance, Felix and Bebe signed up for the *Niles*

Nitkin Total Person mini-course being given at the Bonsai Valley Community Center.

It was during the second lecture, "Talking Things Out," that Felix and Bebe realized that the most meaningful communication they had was when Felix asked each morning, "Where's the Lavoris, honey?" Invariably, Bebe would reply, "Don't look at me."

This was an important revelation. By the end of the mini-course, the "Smiths" reported that Felix had found the Lavoris and that the two of them had reached a real "communication breakthrough." Each was on the road toward becoming a Total Person and, as a dividend, a selfless mate. For Felix, this meant cheerfully foregoing a Saturday afternoon out gigging frogs with his close friend Marty, because he had decided it was more important to "be near" Bebe while she prepared chocolate-covered lady fingers for the Brotherhood Week Bake Sale. For Bebe, it meant learning not to leave the room or trying to change the subject when Felix offered to do his Hugh Downs imitation at parties.

THE NILES NITKIN ANALOGY NUMBER ONE
Felix and Bebe are not an isolated example. Until they began to solve their problems, each was an incomplete person, flawed in at least two dozen ways. Another way of looking at this is for every couple to think of itself as a deck of cards. Ask yourselves: Are all the suits present —spades, diamonds, clubs, and, most important, hearts? Is the deck unfairly "stacked"? Indeed, are the two of you, in the words of our founder, Niles Nitkin, "playing with a full deck"? Does one of you occasionally withdraw from the other, saying "Go fish," when he or she could easily be more resourceful?

WATCH WHAT HAPPENS!
One of the keys to success in the striving toward Total Personhood is to learn spontaneity. When Jim and Sally "Robinson" decided to enroll in the Total Person course, Jim had privately resigned himself to the notion that

Sally was "just no fun." Of course, Jim, who hadn't yet attended the lecture on "Expressing Our True Feelings," hadn't let Sally in on this little secret. When he finally did, Sally at first felt hurt but then determined to remedy the situation by taking a hint from the fifth lecture, "Surprises and Costumes."

Jim came home the next evening with a weary look on his face, the sure sign of another "long day at the office," but he perked up immediately when he saw that Sally was wearing nothing but an old pair of hipboots, which she had "dolled-up" with crepe paper streamers. Was he ever surprised! A couple of nights later, Sally greeted Jim in a getup that Jim agreed made her look "a lot like Donna Reed." And by the end of the week, Jim himself had gotten into the act, surprising Sally by dressing up as a kangaroo.

Soon, young Randy "Robinson" was telling the kids at school that he couldn't wait to get home each night "to see Mom and Dad's neat costumes."

Now that the ice has been broken, Jim frequently changes into his kangaroo outfit before leaving the office, although Sally never knows when he will surprise her, and vice versa. Also, with virtually no advance warning, Sally will often jolt Jim with a wacky suggestion like "Let's go bike riding after dinner!" or "How 'bout taking in a flick tonight?" This is what spontaneity is all about. It's done so much for the "Robinsons" that Jim recently thrilled Sally with the "new" set of snow tires that she had been hinting about for so long.

THE NILES NITKIN ANALOGY NUMBER TWO

Another way of looking at this is for every couple to think of itself as a bacon-lettuce-and-tomato sandwich. Ask yourselves: Are the ingredients in proper balance? Too much lettuce and tomato and not enough bacon? Are the vegetables "fresh and crisp" or "wilted and soggy"? Is there enough mayo—i.e., the "spice of life"? Are you the sort of people who belong in the same sandwich in the first place, or is one of you a "sardine" while the other is "guava paste"? Niles Nitkin says, "You *can* tell a book by its cover. Try to be nice. Adapt."

GETTING ORGANIZED

Every successful organization has a leader—a chairman of the board or president—assisted by several executive vice-presidents. This we know from "management theory," a theory that Niles Nitkin has relied upon in formulating the *Total Person Game Plan*. As a logical extension of management theory, we can see that the person seeking Total-ness, but somehow falling short of fulfillment, is perhaps suffering from poor coordination among his internal corps of executive vice presidents. That's right: Each of us has inside himself a production-unit manager, a marketing-unit manager, a planning-unit manager, and other high-level executives. When these executives work together as a "team," we have harmony. But when there is "corporate in-fighting" or "messy office politics," we experience turmoil.

Frank and Trudy "Jones" had just this sort of turmoil, and it proved costly. The sad truth was that their internal corporate management flow diagrams were radically incompatible. Trudy was deeply committed to long-range planning while Frank was a production-oriented man. Even their closest friends had never suspected this about them. As it was, Frank was so perilously one-sided in his production orientation that he had, in effect, "fired" the top personnel in his marketing and planning departments. Conflict was inevitable. The problem surfaced when Frank and Trudy entered the husband-wife tag-team wrestling tournament at the Elks Club "Fun Night." Their opponents in the first round were Steve and Diane "Crowley."

Before the match, the "Joneses" mapped out a "quick-fall" strategy. It called for Frank to surprise Steve with a fireman's carry and to parlay that into a painful chicken-wing pin hold that would force Steve to "say 'uncle.'" Unfortunately, Steve aggressively "put the good moves" on Frank, bouncing him off the turnbuckle and then bringing him to the mat with a flying figure-four leg scissor around the head. At this point, Trudy could have helped Frank by jumping into the ring and illegally pulling down Steve's trunks. Trudy later claimed that she had actually thought of this, but her weak production orientation had stifled her; she couldn't cope when her "plan" had gone awry. Likewise, Frank's limitations as a "planner" hindered his ability to escape from the grasp of Steve "Crowley," a production and planning dynamo. Ultimately, it was Frank who "said 'uncle.'"

Two incomplete persons can become Total Persons when they intelligently match their strengths in a relationship. All of this is spelled out in Niles Nitkin's eighth lecture, "Cleaning Up One's Act."

THE NILES NITKIN ANALOGY NUMBER THREE
Another way of looking at this is for every couple to think of itself as a brand-new 21" (measured diagonally) color television set. Your equipment might be right and your antenna might be hooked up, but how's the "fine tuning"? Don't expect problems to be self-adjusting. In your dealings with others, are you on the right "wavelength"? Or are you tuned in to "Lowell Thomas Remembers" when everyone around you is stringing along with old Bilko re-runs? Does your future look "bright," or is it clouded with odd-shaped blips? Niles Nitkin says, "Perk up those somber hues! Plug in."

BEING "HAPPY"
There is a special way to become a "happy" Total Person that is touched upon briefly in the Niles Nitkin Total Person lecture series. It is "money." With it, you can become a Total Person just like Sam and Darlene "Jenkins." They reached Total-ity when Darlene hit a number. Niles Nitkin says, "Be happy."

THE NILES NITKIN ANALOGY NUMBER FOUR
Another way of looking at this is for every person to think of himself as a rip-stop nylon mountain tent. Niles Nitkin says, "Got it? O.K. Now you're on your own!"

JAMES STEVENSON

On Labor Day, We Honor the Workingman and His Work

From SOMETHING MARVELOUS IS ABOUT TO HAPPEN by James Stevenson. Copyright © 1971 by James Stevenson. By permission of Harper & Row, Publishers, Inc.

The Javanese
Go-Getter

PITHECANTHROPUS SUDORIFICUS
The First Man to "Work," and a Real Hustler, Too
Skull fragments found in 1937-38 indicate that Pith. Sud. had a brow 6 cm higher than Pith. Erec., suggesting a wide-awake attitude and a heavily furred coccygeal noto-chord (literally "bright-eyed and bushy-tailed"). It is believed that his "work" was primitive in nature—primarily throwing rocks for other people in exchange for bread-fruit.

JAMES STEVENSON

The Stones of Thrud

EARLY WORK—NORWAY
Probable example of prehistoric work. Stones appear to be piled in sequence of size and weight—largest at bottom, smallest at top.

Figure of man resting with cup—Temple of Kukulcan, Chichén Itzá, Mexico

THE COFFEE BREAK
Statuary in Yucatan suggests that Mayan laborers were among first to initiate the "coffee break."

The Unfinished
Horseshoe of the Nile

"GIVING UP"
Before work was fully understood and carried out, there were many attempts—doomed to failure. An example is the famous "Unfinished Horseshoe of the Nile."

VACATION
Once the idea of work was firmly entrenched, man labored three hundred sixty-five days of the year. It was

Ed Burbank, a veteran wattle-wood worker, who conceived the idea of "taking some time off." He returned to the wattle-extract mill after two weeks at his uncle's farm in Ohio.

"Where the hell have *you* been?" demanded the boss.

"I've been on vacation," replied Ed.

"On *what?*"

"Vacation," said Ed, extracting wattle immediately.

"Oh," said the boss. Soon all the workers were taking two weeks off and going to Ed's uncle's farm in Ohio.

Alf

ALF, THE NEWCASTLE
COAL HEAVER
Delivered six wagons of coal to Newcastle, 1851. "Don't blime me," he said. "I owney do as I'm told, see—nuffin' more."

GETTING "PAID"
Etruscan coin (with toothmarks, probably to verify authenticity). Coin discovered in vicinity of early ditch.

DELEGATING WORK
The Egyptian Pharaohs were among the first to understand that the man who conceptualizes the "work" need not be the one to execute it.

HONEST TOIL—
Portion of mural in Oswegatchie, Conn., post office

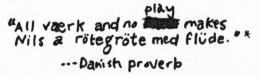

"All værk and no ~~play~~ makes
Nils a rötegröte med flüde."*
---Danish proverb

* Raspberry pudding

ROME—THE FIRST DAY (SUNSET)

Italian construction workers wisely resisted the "speed-up" and refused to complete the city on a rush basis. Their defiance gave courage to future generations of workers, and bequeathed a motto for all times: "Rome wasn't built in a day."

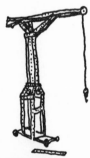

TECHNOLOGY

While playing one day with a six-dollar Meccano set, a distinguished engineer was struck with an idea that would alter the course of history. "If we could make one of these babies really *big*, it could help build things." Soon, huge Meccano cranes and stuff were etched across the sky of America.

LABOR STRIFE

The Battle of Nick's Barbershop, 1919: All Nick's barbers joined the union except old Howard (third chair down), who attempted sabotage by pouring witch hazel on customers' neckties and giving "butches" to everyone who asked for a "light trim."

Philip Rolph at the wheel of his Mack rig

OLDEST UNION MEMBER

Philip Rolph has been a member of the Truckers since 1907. Although ninety-six years old, he is still at the wheel. (His truck, unfortunately, has been stuck in a traffic jam on West 46th Street since last August, and Phil's license has expired.)

Neon

RECALCITRANT MANAGEMENT

Monroe Neon, president of Gibraltar Concrete, swore no union men would ever set foot in his plant. They never did. Union men led a destructive parade through his rhododendrons, however.

ELECTRICITY—GOOD OR BAD?

The advent of electricity has been both a blessing and a curse to the workingman. Many workers have detected slippage in the motivational area, declaring, "Why should *I* do it if electricity can do it?" Indifference and apathy increased after the invention of the dry-cell battery.

MACHINE VS. MAN/THE THREAT OF AUTOMATION

The sharp decline of sweet singers in saloons is traceable to the jukebox (below). This is just one example.

Brutmann,
the Wood-carver of Ghent

OBSOLESCENCE
No sooner had man learned to "work" than he found, to his sorrow, that his "work" was sometimes not wanted. Brutmann, whose rosewood nutcrackers with inlaid elephant-tusk scenes from the Bible were the rage of Ghent, was "laid off" when frescoes caught on big.

DECLINE OF INTEREST IN WORK
Familiar American saying—twentieth century. Suggests that work may be losing some of its appeal.

CALVIN TOMKINS

The Master
of Mill House

By permission of Calvin Tomkins. Copyright © 1973 by Calvin Tomkins.

Clare awoke some time after midnight, her heart pounding and her fine eyes wide with fright. There it was again —the strange sound like distant thunder, coming from the depths of the great house and ending in an ominous, squashy thud. A shiver ran over her delicate, twenty-four-year-old shoulders—deceptively delicate, that is, for Clare was a graduate of the Mountebank School of Physical Therapy, and strong with the sinews of her calling. At the moment, though, she was frightened. The recurrent *thunder-squash-thump,* punctuated every third or fourth time by what sounded like muffled groans,

CALVIN TOMKINS

brought back all the unanswered questions that had nagged her since she arrived, the previous afternoon in that sinister October of 1973, to take up her duties at Mill House.

Why, for example, had she been flown here in a helicopter whose windows were blacked out—blacked out so thoroughly that she could barely read the extra-large print in her paperback gothic novel? She did not even know how far she was from Basking Sump, New Jersey, where she lived with her widowed but plucky mother, or even in what direction they had flown. Was Mill House near the sea? The sound of rushing water had made her think so at first, when they led her, blindfolded, down a corridor to the cozy suite that was to be her combined living quarters and therapy room. But once the door was closed and the blindfold removed she could no longer hear the waves, and when she asked the two neatly dressed and personable young men who had escorted her from the helicopter whether Mill House was near the ocean, the tall, wavy-haired one had merely smiled a lofty smile and walked out. This left her alone with the other, a cleanly barbered fellow, whose eyes, behind aviator glasses, tended to roam altogether too freely over her well-knit yet vulnerable person.

"Well, where's my patient?" she had asked brightly, trying to change what appeared to be the subject. "Where is Mr. Smith?"

"In reply to that," he said, "I would suggest that the advisability of such queries is counterindicated." Whereupon he, too, left the room, locking the door behind him.

"What kind of talk is that?" Clare asked herself now, sitting up in bed and letting the moonlight, through a barred window near the ceiling, stream gratefully over her auburn curls. "And why do I feel this nameless apprehension, this indefinable sense that things are less than right at Mill House? Why, why, why?"

In the morning, though, Clare decided that her fears were groundless. The thumping had stopped. Although she could not see out her window, the light coming through it seemed to be sunny, and breakfast, which was wheeled in by a quite well-mannered Marine sergeant, was full of nutrients.

After breakfast, Clare busied herself in the therapy room, preparing dumbbells, poultices, and, just to be on the safe side, hip baths. She was humming her school song when the tall, wavy-haired man came in and told her to get ready for Mr. Smith. Clare's spirits fairly leaped. At last she was to meet her mysterious employer, the master of Mill House. What would he be like? All she really knew about him was that he was wealthy and important, and that he hurt. She did not even know where he hurt.

Mr. Smith arrived somewhat jerkily a few minutes later, accompanied by an enormous but cringing Irish setter. He was a man of medium height, with bushy red hair, a guardsman's mustache, and reddish chin whiskers. "Hi, there, Mr. Smith," Clare said, in her friendly way. "Where do you hurt?"

"Stfover," Mr. Smith mumbled, through the mustache.

"I beg pardon?"

"He says he's stiff all over," the tall man said.

"Good gracious, you poor thing," Clare said soothingly. Without further ado she picked up Mr. Smith and carried him to the massage table—he was heavier than she expected—and set to work. It was a real challenge, what with the setter alternately licking and snapping at her heels and Mr. Smith flatly refusing to remove even the jacket of his neat, well-cut navy-blue suit, but she did her level best. Mercy me, Clare thought, as she pummelled her patient scientifically, this is the worst case of chronic rigidity I have ever *heard* of.

That afternoon, the man with the aviator glasses invited Clare to play miniature golf. Her first impulse was to refuse. The cool insolence of his manner annoyed and frightened her a little, and yet, somehow, she felt strangely attracted to him. She accepted the invitation, but sulkily. He took her down a long corridor, up some stairs, and through a door that led to an imitation rose garden surrounded by a bulletproof hedge. The imitation rosebushes concealed a clever network of chutes, holes, and labyrinths for golf balls. Clare kept trying to sneak a look through the hedge. Once, she knocked her ball right into the hedge, but when she trotted off to retrieve it her opponent ran after her and pulled her back rather roughly by the hair. Then, before she could realize his intent, he leaned down. She closed her eyes in nervous anticipation of a searing, bureaucratic kiss, but as it turned out, he was only bending to straighten a shoelace. Clare bogeyed the next three holes and returned to her room in a troubled state of mind.

In the next few days, Clare began to feel almost like a prisoner. It was an indefinable sensation, backed by nothing more than the fact that she was kept locked up at all times. She asked the Marine sergeant about it one evening when he brought her supper. "Am I a prisoner here?" she asked, in her forthright way.

"I would answer by saying that I have no information that would lead to such a conclusion," he said. Clare found this reassuring, but still...

Halfway through supper, Clare put down her knife and fork. Usually she had a robust appetite, but this evening it had been spoiled by finding a recording device in the

Boston cream pie. Clare simply *had* to know the truth about Mill House. Was she a prisoner? If so, whose, and was he good-looking?

Slipping the lock on her door with a guitar pick—a technique learned at Mountebank—she ventured out into the dimly lit corridor. She had gone only a few steps when she began hearing again what she had heard the first night—the sound of rushing water. It seemed to come from behind a door up ahead, a door that yielded easily a moment later to her guitar pick. As she stepped hesitantly inside, the sound of roaring and rushing increased greatly in volume. Her hand groped for the light switch and found it. She was in a longish, windowless room that instinct told her must be a laundry, for it was full of washing machines, all going lipperty-lip. Clare bent down to look in the window of the nearest washer. Through the suds, she saw a watery tangle of hundred dollar bills. Who could be washing money at *this* hour?

Scarcely did the question have time to form in her mind when the lights flicked off and eight steely fingers and two thumbs closed around her neck. In the faint glow from the washer dials, it seemed to Clare that the tall, wavy-haired man (for it was he) was bending down to scald her lips with a high-level staff kiss in which the elements of attraction and repulsion were inextricably intertwined, but just at this moment one of the washing machines ceased its churning, and the man straightened up. "*Uh*-oh," he muttered, and began to rummage through his trouser pockets. "You don't happen to have a quarter on you, do you?" he inquired.

Clare lost consciousness.

When she awoke some time later, she was back in her room. She was lying on her bed, and she was clad, to her surprise and chagrin, in her sheerest travel-light nightie. Had she dreamed that frightening encounter? Or, more likely, did *they* want her to *think* she had dreamed it? Clare lay very still, listening to the thump of her heart. Gradually she came to the chilling realization that this was not the only thump to be heard. There it came again—the hideous *thunder-squash-thump*, followed by piteous, stifled groans!

Terrified though she was, Clare knew that she had no choice but to trace the sound to its source. Someone was in pain, perhaps in need of therapy! She rose from bed and tried the door. It was unlocked. For a moment it crossed her mind that this could well be a trap of some insidious sort. She paused picturesquely on the threshold, straining to see down the dark corridor. But then the thunder and the groaning sounded again, and she flew forward on bare but determined feet. The faint *chuff-chuff* of a motorized golf cart told her she was being followed. She ran even faster, down the endless corridor to the flight of stairs. Up or down? The groans seemed to come from below. Clare plunged cellarward.

She groped her way along another, darker corridor, pausing to listen at intervals. The sounds grew louder and more dreadful with every step. Finally, she came to a locked door flanked on either side by an American flag. There was no time for the guitar pick, and besides, she had lost it in the laundry. With a quick, chopping motion of her right hand—the well-known Mountebank Dorsal Reticulater—she soundlessly broke the lock and stepped into a large and splendidly appointed chamber, lit by crystal chandeliers and decorated with busts of Frank Sinatra and the Washington Redskins' front four.

Mr. Smith stood with his back to her, at the head of a mahogany-and-teakwood bowling alley. But wait! *Was* it Mr. Smith? Her fine therapist's eye recognized the stiff, machinelike motions with which the man picked up a ball, tottered back three paces, and then launched himself unsteadily forward, but it was perfectly clear that his hair was neither red nor bushy. The ball hit the alley quite hard, bounced twice, veered to the right, and thundered down the gutter and into the padded backboard—*thunder-squash-thump*. A sob of rage and frustrated executive privilege broke from the bowler. He turned to wipe his hands on a terry-cloth flag, disclosing to Clare features devoid of mustache or beard but suddenly and totally familiar. At this moment, the room filled with fine-looking young bureaucrats in golf carts. The bowler gazed at them with ill-concealed annoyance. "You want me to quit," he said, trying very hard to smile. "But that would be the easy thing. I'm not quitting until I break sixty."

As a dozen upstanding young bureaucrats closed in to seize her, Clare clapped one hand to her still unviolated lips and fainted dead away.

CALVIN TRILLIN

A Nation of Shopkeepers Loses Three of Them Through Contact With a Nation of Violence

First published in The Atlantic Monthly. © 1970 by Calvin Trillin. Reprinted by permission of Calvin Trillin.

CYRIL CRENSHAW, STATIONER, 1905-1970
Crenshaw, a stationer of Knightsbridge, London SW2, perished in the attempt of Harvey R. ("Giveaway") Gordon, a Pontiac dealer from Indianapolis, Indiana, to purchase a ball-point pen. Gordon needed the pen in order to write his congressman that a country whose businessmen had no more initiative than British shopkeepers demonstrated should be cut off Marshall Plan aid immediately.

As the Metropolitan Police pieced the story together, Gordon's irritation at British business methods began on his first evening in London when, trying to relax from the flight over, he attempted to purchase a ticket at a Kensington cinema fourteen seconds after the final showing of the feature film had begun. The ticket seller informed Gordon that the box office was closing. When he tried to press his money upon her, she reminded him that he would not have received a fair return for it anyway, having already missed not only fourteen seconds of credits in the feature film but two trailers for coming attractions, a newsreel featuring a Manchester apprentice school's unique program for training Kenyan welders, and seven minutes of Horlicks advertisements. Gordon—who, on those occasions when he had to work on his books until three or four in the morning at Giveaway Gordon's Garden of Pontiacs, always kept all the showroom lights on just in case an insomniac station-wagon prospect wandered by—stormed into the theater, flinging a handful of coins at the ticket seller. Two police constables later agreed to remove Gordon physically from a seat in the front stalls, on the grounds not only that he entered when the box office was closing but also that he was improperly seated, having flung a total of ten shillings, the price for the loges (plus a house key), at the ticket seller and then taken a seven-shilling seat.

The following morning Gordon appeared to be less hostile. When the proprietor of a Savile Row clothing store warned him that the two-hundred-dollar cashmere sport coat he was about to buy might not wear terribly well, Gordon, who had once persuaded a mildly alcoholic machine-tool heiress to buy a Pontiac with eighty-seven thousand four hundred dollars' worth of extras, merely suggested to the clothier that he seek medical attention. But that afternoon, Gordon himself has admitted, there was another throwing incident, this time involving a greengrocer near Victoria Station. Gordon told the greengrocer that he wanted four peaches, and then began to pick them out.

"I'll get them for you, sir, thanks very much," the greengrocer said.

"That's all right, I'll get them," Gordon replied.

"But you'll take all large ones," the greengrocer said.

"Well, of course I'll take all large ones," Gordon said.

"Well, that's hardly fair to the next chap, is it?" the greengrocer said.

"Fair!" Gordon said. "If you were interested in being fair you should have gone into refereeing."

"We can't all be picking out our own peaches, sir," the greengrocer said, whereupon Gordon picked out four of his own peaches, all large ones, and threw them at the greengrocer. The greengrocer and three of the peaches were bruised.

On the same day, Gordon apparently failed to arrange the mending of a shirt, having been told by one laundry that it didn't do small holes and by the laundry next door that it was not equipped for major mending unless Gordon wanted to book three weeks in advance. Two days later, Gordon threatened violence in a shop—the Minimum Delay Cleaners on Brompton Road. Gordon, noticing that the suit he had just had pressed was about to be taken off the hanger and folded up into a paper bag by the clerk, asked to take the suit on the hanger.

"But we would have to charge you tuppence for the hanger, sir," the clerk replied.

"Sold," said Gordon, who had, within a matter of seconds, calculated that paying tuppence for the hanger would be cheaper in the long run than paying to have the suit repressed after it became wrinkled in the paper bag.

"But you could buy hangers across the road for a penny each, sir," the clerk said.

Gordon stared at the clerk. "I'll give you fourpence for your hanger," he finally said. "But not a penny more."

"Oh, tuppence will be quite all right sir," the clerk said, not quite certain that he had understood Gordon correctly. The clerk then put the suit back on the hanger and started to fold it into the paper bag again. A Mrs. Jeffrey Jowell, who was in the store at the time, has confirmed the clerk's testimony that Gordon snatched the suit from the clerk's hand in a violent motion and, as he threw open the door to leave, threatened the destruction of the shop by arson.

Gordon went directly from the Minimum Delay Cleaners to Crenshaw's stationery shop for a pen, composing the letter in his mind as he walked.

"Terribly sorry, sir," Crenshaw said. "We don't do pens."

"You mean you don't sell them?" Gordon asked.

"I'm afraid not, sir," Crenshaw replied. "Odd—ten, fifteen people a day stop off here wanting to buy pens. I suppose because we sell stationery and greeting cards and all that they expect us to sell pens as well."

"Has it ever occurred to you to begin selling pens?" Gordon said quietly, an odd tightness coming over his voice.

"Oh, no, sir," Crenshaw replied. "We don't do pens."

It was at that point that Gordon reached into his raincoat pocket, pulled out the Magnum automatic he always carried in case anyone came onto the Giveaway Gordon's Garden of Pontiacs lot looking for trouble, and finished off Crenshaw in three quick shots. He later instructed his attorney to base his defense on the claim that the shooting had been a crime of passion.

MARTIN APPLEGATE, NEWS DEALER, 1911-1970
Applegate, a news dealer on Park Lane, was put to death by LeRoy Bean, a millionaire oilman from Ada, Okla-

homa, in the normal course of business. Ironically, the killing was a direct result of Bean's making a special effort to behave courteously to the British. When he wasn't making a special effort to be courteous, Bean made a special effort to be uncouth. He prided himself on his reputation as a crude, self-made wheeler-dealer of the type common in the Southwest—although he was, in fact, a native of Chicago of Latvian descent, a graduate of the University of Illinois in musicology, and a baron of oil only through the happenstance of his wife's father having had control over two hundred and forty-seven million barrels of it.

For years, Bean had been particularly rude to the British, to the intense embarrassment of his wife, who always treated the British with the respect due one's revered ancestors, although all the British she met were live people not related to her. Once, during a reception in Tulsa given by the English Descendants of the Sooner Land Rush, Bean remarked to the British consul that he had by coincidence seen "a whole mess of little-bitty foreigners" downtown that afternoon, knowing full well that the only foreigners who had been downtown were the members of the championship Oxford rugby team who were making a special State Department goodwill tour of eastern Oklahoma. In London, whenever Bean ordered a bartender to bring plenty of ice in his drink, he always added that he realized there were only one hundred seventeen ice cubes in the greater London area at one time. In London restaurants, his orders were always something like, "Bring me one of them chicken pies of yours if you got a crane handy."

After a particularly unpleasant scene in London one night, when Bean insulted the Queen's prize corgi dogs in front of members of the British Natural Gas Association ("Why, in Oklahoma if we ever found a critter that ugly we'd put a bounty on it"), Mrs. Bean announced that if Bean did not make a special effort to be courteous to the British, there would be no more trips out of Ada, a threat she was capable of carrying out, since all of the two hundred and forty-seven million barrels of oil were still in her name.

It was Applegate's bad luck that Bean's first transaction on the morning after Mrs. Bean's dictum was to buy a *Herald-Tribune* on Park Lane. Bean had resolved to be more courteous than the British themselves; the thought of having to spend more than a few months a year in Ada, Oklahoma, surrounded by crude, self-made wheeler-dealers, filled him with dread. Walking down Park Lane, Bean had stopped in front of the Dorchester Hotel's doorman and said, "You got a real fine country here. Real fine." He had decided that at breakfast he would tell the waiter that only the British were intelligent enough to make breakfast sausages mainly out of bread, thus guarding against early-morning heartburn. When he entered Applegate's shop, he said, "A Paris *Herald-Tribune,* please, if you don't mind."

"Thank you," Applegate said. He handed Bean the paper and said "Thank you" again.

"Thank *you*," said Bean, who, after all, had been the one receiving the item in question.

"Thank you very much," Applegate said, as Bean handed him a pound note—and then added, before Bean was able to reply, "Thank you."

"Thanks a lot," Bean said.

"Thanks awfully," Applegate said, handing Bean his change.

"Thank *you*. Thank *you* awfully," Bean said, in a louder voice.

"Thank you very much indeed," Applegate said, somewhat puzzled but trying not to offend a customer.

"Thanks a lot fella—hear?" Bean said. He was almost shouting.

"Thank you, sir," Applegate said. He wondered why Bean was not leaving the store.

"Thank... you... sir... awfully," Bean said, very slowly.

A man in the bakery next door testified that the conversation went for approximately ten minutes before Bean pulled out a long-barreled, pearl-handled revolver—a souvenir his grandfather had come upon during a border skirmish with the Estonians in 1902—and fired at Applegate. The man in the bakery also testified that when the police constables opened the doors of the police van so that Bean could climb in, Bean said, "Thanks awfully."

TIMOTHY PENFOLD,
SWEETSHOP PROPRIETOR, 1902-1970
Penfold, a sweetshop proprietor whose hobby was queuing, had one narrow escape from an American on the same day he eventually met his end at the hands of Myrtle Dougherty of Cleveland Heights, Ohio.

The narrow escape occurred in Penfold's sweetshop. It was a quiet Tuesday morning. Penfold was filling the order of a retired housing inspector who regularly sent a variety of candies in a gift box to the keepers working at a home for worn and misused farm animals in Sussex. It was a complicated order, since the retired housing inspector kept careful notes on the preferences of each keeper, and it often took an hour or so to complete. Penfold and the housing inspector had just spent ten minutes discussing the remarkable fondness of the Deputy Chief Keeper for Mackintosh's Quality Street Toffees when an American walked into the store, picked up a sixpence bag of mixed nuts and raisins from the rack, put a sixpence on the counter in front of Penfold, and said, "OK?"

"Won't keep you a moment, sir," Penfold said to

the American, getting right down to adding an eighteen-inch column of figures.

"I'm just leaving this for the nuts and raisins," the American said. He had started out of the shop but had stopped to look at Penfold for an answer.

"I won't be long here, sir, thank you very much," Penfold said, starting to check each candy bar in the box against the numbers in the column.

"But it's the right change," the American said.

Penfold looked up from his figures. "There's a queue, sir," he said, sternly.

Penfold turned back to his figures, and the American reached into his pocket for a .45-caliber pistol he had been carrying for just such occasions. At that point, by chance, the American's wife walked in, reminded him that mixed nuts were high in cholesterol, and led him from the store.

Unaware of his narrow escape, Penfold decided to spend that evening queuing about. He often spent his evenings that way, joining first one queue then another. He had a closetful of items that he had purchased without really needing them, souvenirs of the times when he had been enjoying himself so much that he neglected to leave the queue before arriving at the counter and had to buy something or risk being accused by those behind him of having queued frivolously. Once, on Regent Street, he had been rather embarrassed when he joined what he thought was a short queue toward a shop door but turned out to be a German tourist ducking out of the wind to light a cigarette. But he continued to find queues irresistible, and he often spent an entire evening strolling from bus stops to cinemas to news dealers and back, queuing happily.

There was nothing frivolous about Penfold's presence in the fatal queue. On closing his sweetshop for the evening, he had decided to go to Hammersmith, where there was an Odeon cinema queue he had always found agreeable. He arrived at the bus stop fully intending to take a Number 74 bus to Hammersmith, although he enjoyed thinking that he was also queuing for the Number 31, which used the same stop. As it happened, there was only one person waiting at the bus stop when Penfold arrived—Mrs. Dougherty, who was returning from a beauty parlor that, according to an article on the women's page of the Cleveland *Plain Dealer*, did the hair of some close friends of Tom Jones, the singer. In Cleveland Heights, Mrs. Dougherty was vice president of her Parent-Teacher Association, recording secretary of the Housewives and Mothers Protection Society Gun Club, and a black belt in karate who had once demonstrated her murderous skill by breaking a Whirlpool washer-dryer with one chop of her bare hand. Penfold stood directly behind Mrs. Dougherty, in the proper queue position. Mrs. Dougherty, sensing someone behind her, moved slightly to the left, in better position if she decided to bring her right elbow back into the assaulter's windpipe. Penfold, not wanting to appear to be breaking the queue, dutifully moved directly behind her again. Mrs. Dougherty moved to the right, and again Penfold moved behind her, silently congratulating himself on attentive queuing. Believing her suspicions confirmed, Mrs. Dougherty faked a left elbow to the lower abdomen, spun around to a kneel-and-fire position, and shot Penfold four times with a small derringer she kept in her passport wallet. Before he expired, Penfold was heard to say, "I hope you don't think I was trying to push ahead."

Jacob Schiff and My Uncle Ben Daynovsky

First published in *Moment*. © 1975 by Calvin Trillin.
Reprinted by permission of Calvin Trillin.

*The silk-hat banker Jacob Schiff, concerned about the
conditions on the East Side of New York (and embarrassed by the image it created for New York's German
Jews), pledged half a million dollars in 1906 to the
Galveston Project, which helped direct more than ten
thousand East European migrants through Galveston
into the South and Southeast.*
—*The Provincials: A History of Jews
in the South,* by Eli N. Evans.

And who is Jacob Schiff that he should be embarrassed

by my Uncle Ben Daynovsky? My father's family certainly came to Missouri from Eastern Europe around 1908 via the port of Galveston, and, I'll admit, that route struck me as rather odd every time we read in history class about how all the tired, poor, huddled masses swarmed into this country through Ellis Island. It never occurred to me, though, to explain it all by assuming that Jacob Schiff found my family not only tired and poor and huddled but also embarrassing. I always considered the Galveston passage to be one of those eccentricities of ancestral history that require no explanation—the kind of incident we hear about so often from people who have family trees concocted for themselves by wily English genealogists ("For some reason, the old boy showed up late for the Battle of Hastings and therefore survived to father the first Duke, and that's why we're here to tell the tale"). I have always been content—pleased, really—to say simply that my grandfather (Uncle Ben's brother-in-law) happened to land in Galveston and thus made his way up the river (more or less) to St. Joseph, Missouri, leaving only sixty miles or so for my father to travel in order to complete what I had always assumed to be one of the few Kiev–Galveston–St. Jo–Kansas City immigration patterns in the Greater Kansas City area.

To be absolutely truthful, it occurred to me more than once that my grandfather and Uncle Ben might have caught the wrong boat. I have never heard my mother's views on the subject, but I have always assumed that she would believe that the use by my father's family of a port no one else seemed to be using had something to do with the stubbornness for which they retain a local renown in St. Jo. As I imagine my mother's imagining it, my grandfather would have fallen into an argument with some other resident of Kiev (or *near* Kiev, as it was always described to me, leading me to believe as a child that they came from the suburbs) about where immigrants land in the United States. The other man said Ellis Island; my grandfather said Texas. When the time came to emigrate, my grandfather went fifteen hundred miles out of his way in order to avoid admitting that he was wrong. My grandfather died before I was born, but my Uncle Ben is still living in St. Jo; he has lived there for sixty or seventy years now, without, I hasten to say, a hint of scandal. Stubborn, O.K. But I simply can't understand how anyone could consider him embarrassing.

"Who is Jacob Schiff that he should be embarrassed by my Uncle Ben Daynovsky?" I said to my wife when I read about the Galveston Project in *The Provincials.*

"You shouldn't take it personally," my wife said.

"I'm not taking it personally; I'm taking if for my Uncle Ben," I said. "Unless you think that Jacob Schiff's descendants are embarrassed by my moving to New York instead of staying in our assigned area."

"I'm sure Jacob Schiff's descendants don't know anything about this," my wife said.

"And who are they they they should be embarrassed by my Uncle Ben Daynovsky?" I said. "A bunch of stockbrokers."

"I think the Schiffs are investment bankers," my wife said.

"You can say what you want to about my Uncle Ben," I said, "but he never made his living as a money-lender."

I'm not quite sure how my Uncle Ben did make his living; I always thought of him as retired. As a child, I often saw him during Sunday trips to St. Jo—trips so monopolized by visits to my father's relatives that I always assumed St. Jo was known for being populated almost entirely by Eastern European immigrants, although I have since learned that it had a collateral fame as the home of the Pony Express. Until a few years ago, Uncle Ben was known for the tomatoes he grew in his backyard and pickled, but I'm certain he never produced them commercially. A few years ago, when he was already in his eighties and definitely retired, Uncle Ben was in his backyard planting tomatoes when a woman lost control of her car a couple of blocks behind his house. The car went down a hill, through a stop sign, over a median strip, through a hedge, and into a backyard two houses down from Uncle Ben's house. Then it took a sharp right turn, crossed the two backyards, and knocked down my Uncle Ben. It took Uncle Ben several weeks to recover from his physical injuries, and even then, I think, he continued to be troubled by the implications of that sharp right turn. One of his sons, my cousin Iz, brought Uncle Ben back from the hospital and said, "Pop, do me a favor: next time you're in the backyard planting tomatoes, keep an eye out for the traffic."

"First that car makes a mysterious right turn and now he's being attacked by a gang of stockbrokers," I said. "It hardly seems fair."

"There's something very interesting about the Schiffs listed in *Who's Who*," I said to my wife not long after our first conversation about the Galveston Project.

"I think you'd better find yourself a hobby," she said.

"As a matter of fact, I'm thinking about taking up genealogy," I said. "But listen to what's very interesting about the Schiffs listed in *Who's Who;* the Schiffs who sound as if they're descendants of Jacob Schiff seem to be outnumbered by some Schiffs who were born in Lithuania and now manufacture shoes in Cleveland."

"What's so interesting about that?"

"Well, if Jacob Schiff thought people from Kiev were embarrassing, you can imagine how embarrassed he must have been by people from Lithuania."

"What's the matter with people from Lithuania?" she said.

"I'm not sure, but my mother's mother was from Lithuania and my father always implied that it was nothing to be proud of," I said. "He always said she had an odd accent in Yiddish. I'm sure he must have been right, because she had an odd accent in English. Anyway, *Who's Who* has more Lithuanian Schiffs than German Schiffs, even if you count Dorothy Schiff."

"Why shouldn't you count Dorothy Schiff?" my wife said. "Isn't she the publisher of the New York *Post?*"

"Yes, but why is it that she is publisher of the New York *Post?*"

"Well, I suppose for the same reason anybody is the publisher of any paper," my wife said. "She had enough money to buy it."

"Only partly true," I said. "She is the publisher of the New York *Post* because several years ago, during one of the big newspaper strikes, she finked on the other publishers in the New York Publishers Association, settled with the union separately, and therefore saw to it that the *Post* survived, giving her something to be publisher of."

"Since when did you become such a big defender of the New York Publishers Association?" my wife said.

"My Uncle Ben Daynovsky never finked on anybody," I said.

"Maybe that passage in *The Provincials* was wrong," my wife said when she came into the living room one evening and found me reading intently. "Maybe Schiff gave the money to the Galveston Project just because he wanted to help people like your grandfather get settled."

"I'm glad you brought that up, because I happen to be consulting another source," I said, holding up the book I was reading so that she could see it was *Our Crowd*, which I had checked out of the library that day with the thought of finding some dirt on Jacob Schiff.

"Here's an interesting passage in this book about some of the German-Jewish charity on the Lower East Side: 'Money was given largely but grudgingly, not out of the great religious principle of *tz'dakah*, or charity on its highest plane, given out of pure loving kindness, but out of a hard, bitter sense of resentment, and embarrassment and worry over what the neighbors would think.'"

"I don't see what you hope to gain by finding out unpleasant things about Jacob Schiff," she said.

"Historical perspective," I said, continuing to flip back and forth between the Jacob Schiff entry in the index and the pages indicated. "Did you know, by the way, that Schiff had a heavy German accent? I suppose when it came time to deal with the threat of my Uncle Ben, he said something like, 'Zend him to Galveston. Zum of dese foreigners iss embarrassink.'"

"I never heard you make fun of anybody's accent before," my wife said.

"They started it."

"My Uncle Ben never associated with robber barons like Gould and Harriman," I said to my wife a few days later. "When it comes to nineteenth-century rapacious capitalism, my family's hands are clean."

My wife didn't say anything. I had begun thinking that it was important that she share my views of Jacob Schiff, but she was hard to convince. She didn't seem shocked at all when I informed her, from my research in *Our Crowd*, that Schiff had a private Pullman car, something that anyone in my family would have considered ostentatious. When I told her that Schiff used to charge people who made telephone calls from his mansion—local calls, I wouldn't argue about long distance—she said that rich people were bound to be sensitive about being taken advantage of. "One time, he was called upon to give a toast to the Emperor of Japan, and he said, 'First in war, first in peace, first in the hearts of his countrymen,'" I said.

"It's always hard to know what to say to foreigners," she said.

"What about the checks?" I said one evening.

"What checks?" she said.

"The checks Schiff had framed on the wall of his office," I said.

"I can't believe he had checks framed on the wall of his office," my wife said.

"I refer you to page one hundred fifty-nine of *Our Crowd*," I said. "Schiff had made two particularly large advances to the Pennsylvania Railroad, and he had the cancelled checks framed on his wall."

"Did he really?" she said, showing some interest.

"One of them was for $49,098,000," I said.

"That is kind of crude," she said.

"Not as crude as the other one," I said. "It was for $62,075,000."

"I think that's rather embarrassing," she said.

"I would say so," I said, putting away the book. "I just hope that no one in St. Jo hears about it. My Uncle Ben would be mortified."

GEORGE TROW

Bobby Bison's Bicentennial Dinner Dance

By permission of George Trow. © 1977 George Trow.

*Will You (The Reader) Be Invited to Bobby Bison's
Bicentennial Dinner Dance?*
Probably not. Bobby Bison's Social Secretary is firm.
"No detrimentals," says Bobby Bison's Social Secretary.
Bobby Bison is sorry that his old friends will not be
allowed to attend his Bicentennial Dinner Dance.

*Will Bobby Bison's Mom and Dad Be Allowed to Attend
Bobby Bison's Bicentennial Dinner Dance?*
Not a chance. Bobby Bison tried to intercede, but his
Social Secretary was firm. Naturally, Bobby Bison is very

unhappy that his Mom and Dad will not be allowed to attend his Bicentennial Dinner Dance.

Will There Be Heavy Security at Bobby Bison's
Bicentennial Dinner Dance?
You bet. Bobby knows that people will go to any lengths to attend his Bicentennial Dinner Dance. For this reason, he has engaged the armed forces of Burma to guarantee the security of his dance. If you (the reader) attempt to crash Bobby Bison's Bicentennial Dinner Dance, the security forces of the Burmese Government will turn you away. *Won't Your Face Be Red!*

Will Bobby's Party Be Shown on Television?
Not in North America.

How Will Bobby Bison's Bicentennial Dinner Dance
Differ from Other Bicentennial Dinner Dances?
Special luxury features not available at other so-called Bicentennial Dinner Parties include:
   * Patriotic hors d'oeuvres.
   * A giant *tableau vivant* depicting events surround-
     ing the enactment of the legendary "Tariff of
     Abominations."
   * A Eugene V. Debs look-alike contest.
   * Individual ramekins of parsley butter imprinted
     with the seal of one of the thirteen original
     "states."
   * Courtesy crackers.
In addition, mittens of purest lamb's wool will be distributed on a first-come, first-serve basis. Later there will be dancing. That's all Bobby wants to tell you now.

Has Bobby Bison Forgotten His Old Friends?
Bobby has arranged for the text of his guest list to be serialized in leading women's magazines, but he understands that for his very closest friends (including his Mom and Dad), this will not be enough.

That is why Bobby has instructed the Bobby Bison Mint to strike up a special Commemorative Issue of Plausible Medallions depicting scenes from his Bicentennial Dinner Dance as it will be experienced by the partygoers themselves.

Bobby Bison Wishes You Could See These Plausible Representations of His Bicentennial Dinner Dance
Look. Look at their metal-like beauty. It's too bad you can't see them. No expense, or almost no expense, has been spared. *Turn them over in your hand*. See, they have *weight*. Also length and breadth. Look at their beautiful *circumference*—see how each medallion takes its inspiration from a well-known geometric figure. *Measure the radius*: yes, your medallions have a *radius*, just like medallions costing much, much more. It's such a shame you can't see them.

The Total Keepsake comprises Five Plausible Scenes from Bobby Bison's Bicentennial Dinner Party:
1. "Tariff of Abominations"
2. "Dancing"
3. "Mittens"
4. "The Spirit of American Cookery"
5. "Heavy Security"

You (The Reader) Have Been Pre-Selected by the Acceptance Committee of the Bobby Bison Mint to Be a Keepsake Trainee.
To simplify matters, your election has already been held. Your bill is being typed right now. Bobby's Social Secretary is standing by to make sure everything goes smoothly. FOR ALL WE KNOW, YOUR KEEPSAKE MEDALLIONS COULD BE APPRECIATING IN VALUE THIS VERY SECOND. There. Your bill has been typed. All done. That was quick. To simplify matters, your Bobby Bison Trust Officer will call on you in the morning.

People Are...

First published in the *National Lampoon*. © 1970 George Trow.
Reprinted by permission of George Trow.

People Are Absolutely Dying . . . to crash the tiny, tiny little dinners Principe Romulus de Remus gives for the most important people in Europe. Il Principe (who comes from *the* oldest Roman family) is Secretary General of the League of Nations. The League is doing reams of important work *in a quiet way*, unraveling prickly plebiscite problems left over from World War I (*the* war as far as everyone rich and chic in Europe is concerned), and his many, many diplomatic duties scarcely leave the Principe an ounce of time to devote to his billion-dollar (or is it lira?) cosmetic empire.

People Are Frantic With Worry . . . about Cleo Moore, whom no one has seen since the middle 1950s. Cleo's

201

the big blonde (everyone loved her) who made her name as "The Long Kiss Girl" by kissing people for minutes and hours on end. *Plus ça change....* We happen to know that Cleo, who's very much into the whole exciting Women's Liberation thing these days, has had her lips removed as her own *very personal* protest against masculine exploitation and is now living in seclusion in Boca Raton, Fla.

People Are Surprised . . . at how quickly the whole Black Power-Civil Rights balloon burst.... *We're* not.... All that talk-talk-talk about "oppression"—so negative, so shrill, so *unfun.* Too bad, because *properly promoted,* that divine black skin could have become *fashion law.*

People Are Talking About . . . crime, petite crime, street crime, up-tight, middle-of-the-night crime . . . LATEST FLASH—absolutely too thrilling to ram through the chic-quest store in town (where you have an impeccable charge, *of course!)* and simply slather yourself all over with *shoplifted goodies....* Unbreakable Rule: Don't take a thing you really truly want. If you get caught (too amusing), you just charge it all and return it the next day. If you get away scot-free-as-a-bird, use your "haul" for stockingstuffers—or chuck it down the garbage disposal.

People Are Reviving . . . our priceless religious heritage. Buy a starched *nun's habit* white-as-the-snow with just a heavenly *hint* of an empire waist—or an antique reliquary studded with jewels just too precious.... Break the trust wide open and splurge on an old church (any denomination but Lutheran will do) that can be moved piece by sacred piece to the Hamptons and used as a beach house.... Invite a minister (Episcopalian is nicest) to dinner and make him recite those charming, old-as-the-hills *creeds and blessings.* It's freaky, *but people are doing it!*

People Are Talking About . . . Jean-Claude Lunch, 76, curly gray hair, stands straight as a ramrod, from the oldest family in Bruges, and absolutely, unpredictably VIOLENT. His book, *The Theatre of the Whip*, swims in every mind truly devoted to theater and anti-theater. If you are in Bruges, a small fortune (and a raft of references from such people as Principe Romulus de Remus) will get you tickets to Lunch's staging of *Death of a Salesman*, the only play our Jean-Claude regards as worth the trouble. Sometimes, he puts members of the very small, very select audience in great vats of cream. As they thrash around, the cream turns to butter. It's freaky, *but people are doing it!*

People Are Flocking . . . to Dr. Rudolph Bentworsky, a precious poltergeist of a Pole who is simply *redoing* the eyes of everyone enviable you've ever envied. Contessa Porsena (the chic sister of Principe Romulus de Remus) floored everyone at the Bruges premiere of Jean-Claude Lunch's *Death of a Salesman* when she arrived after having her *eyelids icicled* by Dr. Bentworsky. In this short, painless operation, Dr. Bentworsky singes off the natural growth of eyelash with a blowtorch; then, in a special "deep cold" room in his Upper East Side town house, he carefully uses an eyedropper to place tiny drops of liquid on the scarred lid. Sooner or later, beautiful little icicles begin to form on the scar tissue and the effect is. . .magic!

People Are Captivated by . . . Emile Durkheim, society's newest cult figure. Emile's best-selling *Le Suicide* is on every credenza and prie-dieu. Emile's unique importance lies in the fact that he believes that religion and morality originate in the collective mind of society, which is quite amusing if you stop to think about it. *People are wondering* whether Emile and the vivacious Mme. Durkheim will be staying at the Palm Beach house of Mrs. Stephen (Laddie) Sanford again this winter, or whether they'll stay in their beloved Paris, where Emile is legally dead.

JOHN UPDIKE

Minutes of the Last Meeting

First published in *Audience*. © 1972 by John Updike.
Reprinted by permission of John Updike.

The Chairman of the Committee again expressed his desire to resign.

The Secretary pointed out that the bylaws do not provide for resignation procedures, they provide however for a new slate of officers to be presented annually and a new slate of officers was being accordingly presented.

The Chairman responded that however on the new slate his name was again listed as Chairman. He said he had served since the founding of the Committee and sincerely felt that his chairmanship had become more of a hindrance than a help. He said that what the committee

JOHN UPDIKE

needed at this point was new direction and a refined sense of purpose which he could not provide, being too elderly and confused and out of sympathy with things. That the time had come either for younger blood to take over the helm or possibly for the Committee to disband.

The Secretary pointed out that the bylaws do not provide for disbandment.

In answer to a query from the Chairman, Mrs. Hepple on behalf of the Nominating Sub-Committee explained that the Sub-Committee felt as a whole that the Chairman was invaluable in his present position, that support in the wider community would be drastically weakened by his resignation, and that the nomination of two vice-chairmen and the creation of appropriate sub-committees would effectively lighten his work load.

The Chairman asked how often the Nominating Sub-Committee had met. Mrs. Hepple responded that due to the holiday season they had convened once, by telephone. There was laughter. In the same humorous spirit the Chairman suggested that the only way he could effectively resign would be to die.

Mr. Langbehn, one of the newer members, said before presuming to participate in this discussion he would be grateful for having explained to him the original purposes and intents of the Committee.

The Chairman answered that he had never understood them and would be grateful himself.

Miss Beame then volunteered that though the youngest Founder present she would offer her impressions which were that at the founding of the Committee their purpose was essentially the formal one of meeting to give approval to the activities of the Director. That without the magical personality and earnest commitment of the Director they would not have been gathered together at all. That beyond appointing him Director the bulk of the business at the first meeting had centered upon the name of the Committee, initially proposed as the Tarbox Betterment Committee, then expanded to the Committee for Betterment and Development of Human Resources. That the Director had then felt that the phrase Equal Opportunity should also be included, and perhaps some special emphasis on youth as well, without appearing to exclude the senior citizens of the community. Therefore the title of Tarbox Committee for Equal Development and Betterment for Young and Old Alike was proposed and considered.

Dr. Costopoulos, a Founder, recalled that the Director did not however wish the Committee to appear to offer itself as a rival to already extant groups like the Golden Agers and the Teen Scene and had furthermore regretted in the official committee title any indication of a pervasive ecological concern. So a unanimous vote was taken to leave the name of the Committee temporarily open.

Mrs. Hepple added that even though the Director had been rather new in town it all had seemed a wonderful idea, he was obviously the kind of young man who made things happen.

Mrs. MacMillan, a new member, asked where the Director was.

Miss Beame explained that the Director had vanished after the founding meeting.

Leaving behind a cardboard suitcase and an unpaid phone bill, the Chairman volunteered. There was laughter.

The Secretary pointed out that the bylaws perfectly clearly specify the purpose of the Committee and read excerpts spelling out that "no political candidates or partisan causes should be publicly espoused," "no stocks or bonds were to be held with the objective of financial profit or gain," and "no gambling or licentious assignation would be permitted on any premises leased or owned entirely or in part by the said Committee."

Mr. Langbehn asked to see the bylaws.

The Secretary graciously complied.

Mr. Langbehn claimed after examination that this was a standard form purchasable in any office supplies or stationery store.

Mrs. Hepple said she didn't see that it made any difference, that here we all were and that was the main point.

Mrs. MacMillan inquired as to why the Committee kept meeting in the absence of the Director.

The Treasurer interrupted to ask the evening's Hostess, Mrs. Landis, if it were time for refreshments to be served.

The Reverend Mr. Trussel asked if he might attempt to elucidate the question asked by the good Mrs. MacMillan. He said that at first the Committee had met in the expectation that the Director would reappear and then, in later sessions, as a board of inquiry into where the Director had gone. Finally, they had continued to meet because, in his opinion, they had come to love and need one another.

Miss Beame said she thought that was a touching and true description.

Mrs. Hepple said she didn't see where any of it mattered at this point because not only were most of the Founders in attendance but many new members as well. That the membership had grown instead of withering away as one would suppose if the Committee were entirely dependent upon the Director who for that matter she had quite forgotten what he looked like.

Mr. de Muth volunteered that he had come on to the Committee in his capacity as a social science teacher because he understood at that time there had been under consideration a program to arrange a lecture series or series of happenings on the theme of betterment of resources at the public schools.

Mr. Tjadel said he had come on in his capacity as a tree surgeon because of the ecology angle.

Mrs. MacMillan said she had been given the impression her interest in oral contraception might be applied by the Committee to the town drinking water.

The Chairman stated it was all a muddle and again offered his resignation.

The Secretary pointed out that all of these projects had been under consideration and as far as she was concerned still were.

Mr. Langbehn began to speak.

The Treasurer interrupted to compliment Mrs. Landis on the quality of her refreshments.

Mr. Langbehn thanked all present for bearing with him and filling him in so thoroughly. He said that though none of the projects described had apparently come to fruition he nevertheless did not feel that the members of the Committee including himself should entertain the illusion that their efforts were in vain. That on the contrary they had created much talk and interest in the wider community and that just the fact that they continued to attract to membership such distinguished and varied citizens as those present negated any idea of failure.

[Several sentences missed here due to accident spilling glass.—Sec.]

That what was needed was not any long-term narrowing of the horizons established by the Director but a momentary closer focus upon some doubtless limited but feasible short-term goal within the immediate community.

Mrs. Hepple suggested that a dance or rummage sale be held to raise funds so such a goal might be attacked.

Miss Beame thought that a square dance would be better than a black-tie dance so as to attract young people.

The Chairman moved that the bylaws be amended so as to permit the Committee to disband.

No one seconded.

Mr. Tjadel said he didn't see why there was all this worrying about human resources, in his opinion they had a fine human resource right here in this room. If the trunk is solid, he said, the branches will flourish. There was laughter and applause.

The Treasurer volunteered that in his opinion this was the best meeting yet and that to make itself more effective the Committee should meet more often.

Miss Beame said her heart went out to the Chairman and she thought his wishes should be respected.

The Secretary pointed out that they were respected.

Reverend Mr. Trussel moved that the board of officers as presented by the Nominating Sub-Committee be accepted with the proviso that the Chairman be nominated as Chairman pro tem and that to assist his labors further a Sub-Committee on Goals and Purposes be created, with Mr. Langbehn and Miss Beame as co-chairmen.

Mrs. Hepple and others seconded.

The affirmative vote was unanimous.

ANDREW WARD

The Captain Ephraim Pettifog House/Windfall, Massachusetts/ Open Thursdays, May 12th to June 2nd/by Appointment Only

Copyright © 1975, by The Atlantic Monthly Company, Boston, Mass. Reprinted with permission.

Welcome to the Captain Ephraim Pettifog House. Before we go in, let us pause here on the puckery and consider the early life of the man whose home we have come to visit.

Captain Pettifog was descended from a family of gimcracks who first came to this country in 1658 to escape the oak wilt which was then ravaging their native Wales. The family settled in Windfall, and here, on Ember Friday, 1745, Ephraim was born. "So Faire is hee," his father wrote that night in his daybook, "that Hee woulde make the Hoodwink swoon."

213

Ephraim would inherit his father's way with words, and early on showed signs he was cut out for higher things than gimcrackery. One of the few Pettifog childhood anecdotes which has filtered down to us has Ephraim parboiling some jackdaw while his father labored in the mill. "Isn't that jackdaw cooked yet?" his mother called from the hutch. "Not yet," Ephraim replied. "It's still curdy."

At nineteen, Ephraim ran away from home and took a job as a grip on the trading scudder *Goodernatch*. Four days out of Boston, the carboy succumbed to the flicker and Ephraim took on his duties—keeping tabs and sponging down the offal. Over the next few years Ephraim rapidly rose in station until, on Maytide, 1768, he became the company's youngest captain. His spiff, the *Albacore*, was, as a contemporary chronicler described it, "Fleete as a Foote," and took Ephraim far from his humble beginnings. In West Africa he befriended tribal chieftains and, in return for their kindnesses, brought numerous of their subjects back with him for education and uplift in America's sunny southern colonies.

Captain Pettifog's reputation grew as his wares swept the colonies—from hand-latticed curvets to portable cucking stools from the bustling island of Japan. Having thus accrued considerable wealth, he took a wife, one Henna Scardapane, of the Vermont Scardapanes. "Oh, Mother, ye woulde Love her!" Ephraim wrote of his bride-to-be. "What oil cakes! What nates!"

Which brings us, at last, to the house itself. Built by Ephraim for his new wife in 1772, it is, as you can see, a classic of its period. From quoin to nooky we have endeavored to maintain the house just as it might have been when the Pettifogs resided here. The wings, of course, housing our gift shop, snack bar, and informative ticket office, are new additions, though they were built according to eighteenth-century carpenters' specifications by our own Rozzo Brothers Construction Company.

Let's go in, shall we?

Here in the main sequester, guests would arrive in their finest faddle and pantywaist for the balls and banquets for which the Pettifog House was justly famed. Let me just switch on the tape here. There we are.

The polka you are hearing was one of the Captain's favorites, and local musicians, perched topbeam along the canniken, played it whenever the Captain took to the floor. For most of the week, this room, with its silken balderdash and ornately tucked bedplates, went largely unused. But when ball and banquet time came around, the room was the center of gay and boisterous festivity.

Here on this drop-leaf beggary guests would snack on backslap and outdates, hefty slices of beefwood garnished with finely chopped swit, all washed down with steaming beakers of hubbub. Makes your mouth water, doesn't it?

I'll bet a lot of you have a picture of your colonial forebears as stern old stiffs, but believe me, they knew how to have a good time. They played such parlor games as Catch-As-Catch-Can and Trip-the-Gimp, gathered around this double-fretted payola to sing "What Say the Fipple Flute," and "Take Up the Slack, Mona," and danced the sedate woebegone, the daring piggyback, and the outlandish barramunda.

Now, mind your heads as we go into the kitchen. Remember, the average man's height in the eighteenth century was only four-foot-two.

The kitchen was the true center of the colonial household. Here the day would begin. Henna would arise at one in the morning to begin the breakfast preparations as the menfolk stalked out to do their chores. A daughter would stoke the barbells and gather pinspots for the hearth while sons fed the livestock and dragged postholes through the acreage. If there was any Indian fighting to be done, everyone would try to get it out of the way before the breakfast boom was sounded. Then the family would stand around this signed Heckinlively and feast of bowls of postpone, dapple, and miniken pie.

Incidentally, beneath where you're standing is the hidden Indian stairway we discovered while restoring the house. Nearby we have found artifacts left by the Indians who hid here, off and on, until central heating was installed in 1953.

The colonial housewife did everything over the kitchen hearth: it served her as cooking stove, baking oven, candle dip, die cast, privy, trash compactor, and pop-up toaster. Of course, she lacked the modern conveniences we take for granted today—Cling Free, Spray 'n' Vac—but she did have a few gadgets handy which cut her work time down.

I bet none of you know what this is. Any guesses? No, it's a buckelpitter. See? Couldn't you kick yourselves? You'd put your buckle here, like so, on the prong, turn the crank, and the little blade would snap against it, chucking the pits from your buckles. Over here is another ingenious little invention we would do well to revive. That's right, it's a quacksalver. You'd take your leavings, rinds, girt, what-have-you, dump them down the flout, heat, pull the lever, and out would come your week's supply of sackbut.

One more item I wouldn't want you to pass by— the bathbrick. Looks simple enough, doesn't it? Like an ordinary brick? Well, never sell the bathbrick short. It had a wide range of uses, from crushing puffballs for winter storage to weighing down milady's mobcap.

Now, if you'll just follow me up here to the Captain's library. Here Captain Pettifog could shut himself away from the petty concerns of the household and feast on the works of Brit, Hume, Gold, and Fizzdale. It was here he met with the Bullymuckers to write his famous Landfill Compact, which proposed recreational zoning as a means of ridding the colonies of the hated British. Unfortunately, owing to insufficient postage, the Compact never reached the Continental Congress, and the cause would never benefit fully from the Captain's wise counsel.

Down the hall here is the Captain's bedroom, where he and Henna, upon this prow-shaped bed, were to conceive over thirty-seven children, thirty-four of whom were to perish in infancy from swamp pox, wrist blight, and the sting of the barfly. Over the bed hangs a portrait of Henna's father, the Reverend Root Scardapane, painted by Mosely during one of his frequent blue periods. The rod hanging over the window is a clodpoll, with which the captain could reach down and awaken slumbering sluffers and potluckies in the fields.

The chest here is not original with the house, but from its pugmarkings we have been able to ascertain that it is of the general style, region, and period of Captain Pettifog. Note the flayed clappers, the hand-nudged gloss of its overcoating, the Greek Revival underlap of its emphatically fluted knouts.

The house, by the way, contains not a single nail. Nails, as you know, were not mass produced in the eighteenth century, and it took teams of blacksmiths many weeks to produce one. The house is entirely constructed of roasted chestnut and pushpins, which accounts, I think, for its remarkable durability.

And now the last and, for me, most poignant room in the Pettifog House—the widow's walk. Are we all going to fit?

From here, Henna would watch for the *Albacore's* sails to appear, heralding her husband's return. Sadly, since the house stands some thirty miles inland, Henna never once caught sight of a ship, and eventually died— it is said—of a broken heart, on Mooncleft Eve, 1804, while her husband cruised the Winnebagoes gathering kinksleeve for the nation's cupboards.

ANDREW WARD

Years later, at a community bleed, Captain Petti-fog—patriot, adventurer, and prolific penster to the end—succumbed to a bout of the killjoy. In a ceremony befitting his position and accomplishments, Captain Pettifog was buried in his uniform beside his wife, beneath the snack bar.

This concludes our tour of the Captain Ephraim Pettifog House. We hope you've enjoyed this little journey into our nation's storied past. To exit, just follow the arrows and depart through the powdery to the gift shop, where I urge you to pick up a few of our Pettifog House mementos—clodpoll swizzle sticks, Landfill Compact placemats, and our own factory-fresh pinkroot preserves.

Thanks for coming.

WILLIAM ZINSSER

A Connoisseur's Guide to H$_2$O

First published in *Life.* © 1971 by William Zinsser.
Reprinted by permission of William Zinsser.

Any connoisseur must be gratified (as I am) by the national boom in bottled water, sales of which are expected to reach $150 million this year, double the previous figure. Clearly Mr. and Mrs. America are saying that they are "sick and tired" of water which tastes of chemicals. They want water that tastes good.

How sad, therefore, that so few of my countrymen have any real knowledge of the nuances of bottled water —those subtle factors of soil and vintage which make the *eau naturelle* of one region full-bodied and robust, while the water from a valley just half a mile away will be diffident and unprepossessing.

Let me cite an example from my own cellar, which,

incidentally, is in my attic. In May of 1968, a very good year for water, I took 30 liters from the Naugatuck River in Connecticut, 2.7 miles south of Seymour, choosing the west bank after extensive tasting because the wind on that side, blowing through the chinks of a stone wall, gave the water (though wet) a dry quality that was highly pleasing—assertive but not bombastic. I bottled it with care (for a great water can be lost through indifferent corking), labeled it Naugatuck Brut, and served it successfully to my guests in the fall of 1970, by which time it showed excellent maturation.

Last spring I returned to the same site, only to find that the water had assumed a hint of phosphate, albeit faint, which violated not only its charm but its integrity as a classic *eau sec*. I discovered that a housing development had since been built one mile to the north; hence the residual presence of detergents in the water and a consequent slight carbonation.

Now I am not saying that a water with an intimation of phosphate cannot be graceful or even, on occasion, elegant. I recall a sparkling *Château Deterga-Sol* that I took in 1965 from a stream near Levittown, Pa., which, while lacking the finesse of, say, the noble *Sudzo Premier Cru* of 1962, had an honest aggressiveness that one could scarcely help but find amusing. In general, however, these waters tend to be more bubbly than the discriminating palate could wish. I need only mention the *Schloss Kleenzo* taken last summer from the Hutchinson River near Co-Op City in the Bronx.

What I *am* saying is that one must know one's ecology. How often do we hear, for example, that a person enjoys "bourbon and branch water," little stopping to think about the water—so intent are we on the bourbon! —or to ask why one branch water is illustrious and another merely entertaining. Obviously it depends on what kind of branch is put in the water. A hickory branch will give the water a different bouquet from an oak branch. To put it in lay terms, we might perhaps say that one water will have a suggestion of hickory and the other a suggestion of oak. (I will not deal here with the matter of acorns.)

I am often asked by readers of my column in *Water* magazine: where do I go collecting? Broadly speaking, there are three sources in addition to rivers and lakes—tap water, rainwater and distilled water.

With respect to tap water, the main thing to remember is that it can be obtained from any tap (or faucet). Therefore when I travel in America I am always on a gustatory lark. How well I remember my first sip of water after checking into a motel near Salt Lake City. I could hardly believe my palate. Here was a water that was impetuous in its salinity yet never arrogant. I bottled 12 quarts of this enchanting discovery and have since found it a delightful table companion—ideal, incidentally, with shellfish. But another man might prefer the *Haute Chlorine* of Los Angeles or the modest yet somehow ingratiating *Fluoride Rosé* of Scarsdale. Each to his own taste, as the French say—in French, of course.

In the case of rainwater, you must always ask: what is the water falling *through?* I have a rainwater from Gary, Ind., which exhibits the enormous body typical of a water that contains pig iron particulates, yet it lacks the warm, sooty quality of a rainwater taken in the coal regions of Pennsylvania.

The distilled waters likewise have their own personality and message. I myself am partial to several of the waters now used by filling stations for car batteries, notably the *Sunoco 1967,* which is starting to show greatness, or the interesting little *Esso Fumé* that goes so well with beef stroganoff. Just think: only five years ago few would have dared to serve anything with stroganoff but an Evian or a Perrier.

Jury Duty

First published in *Life*. © 1968 by William Zinsser.
Reprinted by permission of William Zinsser.

JURY DUTY AGAIN. I'm sitting in the "central jurors' room" of a courthouse in lower Manhattan, as I do every two years, waiting to be called for a jury, which I almost never am. It's an experience that all of us have known, in one form or another, as long as we can remember: organized solitude.

The chair that I sit in is a little island of apartness. I sit there alone, day after day, and I go out to lunch alone, a stranger in my own city. Strictly, of course, I'm not by myself. Several hundred other men and women sit on every side, as closely as in a movie theater, also waiting to be called for a jury, which they almost never are. Sometimes we break briefly into each other's lives, when we get up to stretch, offering fragments of talk to fill the emptiness. But in the end each of us is alone, withdrawn into our newspapers and our crossword puzzles and our sacred urban privacy.

The room intimidates us. It is a dreary place, done in thirties Bureaucratic, too dull to sustain more than a few minutes of mental effort. On the subconscious level, however, it exerts a strong and uncanny hold. It is the universal waiting room. It is the induction center and the clinic; it is the assembly hall and the office where forms are filled out. Thoughts come unbidden there, sneaking back from all the other moments—in the army, at camp, on the first day of school—when we were part of a crowd and therefore lonely.

The mere taking of roll call by a jury clerk will summon back the countless times when we have waited for our name to be yelled out—loud and just a little wrong. Like every person whose job is to read names aloud, the jury clerk can't read names aloud. Their shapes mystify him. They are odd and implausible names, as diverse as the countries that they came from, but surely the clerk has met them all before. *Hasn't* he? Isn't that what democracy—and the jury system—is all about? Evidently not.

We are shy enough, as we wait for our name, without the extra burden of wondering what form it will take. By now we know most of the variants that have been imposed on it by other clerks in other rooms like this, and we are ready to answer to any of them, or to some still different version. Actually we don't want to hear our name called at all in this vast public chamber. It is so private, so vulnerable. And yet we don't want to *not* hear it; for only by hearing it are we reassured of our identity, really certain that we are known, wanted, and in the right

place. Dawn over Camp Upton, 1943: Weinberg, Wyzan-
ski, Yanopoulos, Zapata, Zeccola, Zinsser...

I don't begin my jury day in such a retrospective
state. I start with high purpose and only gradually slide
into mental disarray. I am punctual, even early, and so is
everybody else. We are a conscientious lot—partly because we are so surrounded by the trappings of justice,
but mainly because that is what we are there to be. I've
never seen such conscientious-looking people. Observ-
ing them, I'm glad that American law rests on being
judged by our peers. In fact, I'd almost rather be judged
by my peers than judged by a judge.

Most of us start the day by reading. Jury duty is
America's gift to her citizens of a chance to catch up on
"good" books, and I always bring *War and Peace*. I
remember to bring it every morning and I keep it handy
on my lap. The only thing I don't do is read it. There's
something about the room . . . the air is heavy with immi-
nent roll calls, too heavy for tackling a novel that will
require strict attention. Besides, it's important to read
the newspaper first: sharpen up the old noggin on
issues of the day. I'm just settling into my paper when
the clerk comes in, around ten-twenty-five, and calls the
roll ("Zissner?" "Here!"). Suddenly it is 1944 and I am at
an army base near Algiers, hammering tin to make a hot
shower for Colonel McCloskey. That sort of thing can
shoot the whole morning.

If it doesn't, the newspaper will. Only a waiting
juror knows how infinite the crannies of journalism can
be. I read "Arrival of Buyers," though I don't know what
they want to buy and have nothing to sell. I read "Soybean Futures," though I wouldn't know a soybean even
in the present. I read classified ads for jobs that I didn't
know were jobs, like "keypunch operators." What keys
do they punch? I mentally buy 4bdrm 1½bth splt lvl
homes w/fpl overlooking Long Island Sound and dream

of taking ½bath there. I read dog news and horoscopes ("bucking others could prove dangerous today") and medical columns on diseases I've never heard of, but whose symptoms I instantly feel.

It's an exhausting trip, and I emerge with eyes blurry and mind blank. I look around at my fellow jurors. Some of them are trying to work—to keep pace, pitifully, with the jobs that they left in order to come here and do nothing. They spread queer documents on their knees, full of graphs and figures, and they scribble on yellow pads. But the papers don't seem quite real to them, or quite right, removed from the tidy world of filing cabinets and secretaries, and after a while the workers put the work away again.

Around twelve-forty-five the clerk comes in to make an announcement. We stir to attention: we are needed! "Go to lunch," he says. "Be back at two." We straggle out. By now the faces of all my fellow jurors are familiar (we've been here eight days), and I keep seeing them as we poke around the narrow streets of Chinatown looking for a restaurant that isn't the one where we ate yesterday. I smile tentatively, as New Yorkers do, and they smile tentatively back, and we go our separate ways. By one-fifty-five we are seated in the jurors' room again, drowsy with Chinese food and American boredom —too drowsy, certainly, to start *War and Peace*. Luckily, we all bought the afternoon paper while we were out. Talk about remote crannies of journalism!

Perhaps we are too hesitant to talk to each other, to invite ourselves into lives that would refresh us by being different from our own. We are scrupulous about privacy—it is one of the better gifts that the city can bestow, and we don't want to spoil it for somebody else. Yet within almost every New Yorker who thinks he wants to be left alone is a person desperate for human contact. Thus we may be as guilty as the jury system of not putting our time to good use.

What we want to do most, of course, is serve on a

jury. We believe in the system. Besides, was there ever so outstanding a group of jurors as we, so intelligent and fairminded? The clerks have told us all the reasons why jurors are called in such wasteful numbers: court schedules are unpredictable; trials end unexpectedly; cases are settled at the very moment when a jury is called; prisoners plead guilty to a lesser charge rather than wait years for a trial that might prove them innocent. All this we know, and in theory it makes sense.

In practice, however, somebody's arithmetic is wrong, and one of America's richest assets is being dribbled away. There must be a better way to get through the long and tragic list of cases awaiting a solution—and, incidentally, to get through *War and Peace.*

Peabody's Complaint

First published in *The New York Times Book Review.*
© 1970 William Zinsser. Reprinted by permission of William Zinsser.

This is one of those days when I almost wish I were not a literary critic. How can one hope in a brief book review to assess the merits—indeed, the incalculable influence —of a novel which dares, as *Peabody's Complaint* so brilliantly does, to shoulder the whole heavy burden of white Anglo-Saxon Protestant guilt and to reduce it at the end, with a comic flip of the wrist that would be hilarious if it were not so sad, to a mere bag of exploded myths? With this self-mocking yet strangely purgative journey into the WASP gestalt, author Winthrop Bradford has made it well-nigh impossible for other writers who deal in the upper-class Protestant milieu—one thinks of Louis Auchincloss—ever to work this territory again. *Peabody's Complaint*, which I am tempted to call a masterpiece, is the ultimate novel of the WASP's Puritan morality at war with the stirrings of a repressed libido.

Much, of course, has already been written about the book as a publishing "event": the $125,000 advance, the $175,000 paperback contract, the $250,000 sale to a motion picture company. There have also been reports—ever since two chapters appeared last year in *Boys' Life*—about the explicit language that the author uses to describe the erotic fancies of his protagonist, Goodhue Peabody, Jr. I can only say that the rumors are true; this reviewer, at least, has never seen the new permissiveness carried to such an extreme. Typical, perhaps, is the scene in which Peabody recalls being sent to dancing class at the age of ten and having an insatiable desire to pull off the white gloves of his partner, Dee-Dee Fahnestock:

Finally I could control my hands no longer, and I still remember the frightened look in Dee-Dee's eyes when I took hold of her glove—it was the left one—and began to slide it off. I felt the soft satin yield beneath my fingers. Then, unaccountably, something stopped me. I wish I could say—for even today the memory fills me with a shame which is not, however, unmixed with lust—that it was my Puritan conscience tightening the rein on my unbridled id, as, God knows, it had so many times before and would again. But what actually stopped me was that I couldn't get the glove off because the damn thing went several inches above the elbow. Oh, the hot tears of frustration I shed that night for being born into a social class where the girls go muffled in organdy!

Permissive? Of course. There's no denying the

initial shock of seeing words like "organdy" in print. But only a prude would question Bradford's artistic right to let his characters talk with such unflinching candor. For thereby he has found exactly the right tone, it seems to me, to express his own agonized search into the subsoil of American manners for the twisted root-causes of Protestant self-flagellation.

The plan of the book is simple. It takes place in the rectory of the Episcopal Church of Saint Edward the Confessor (a not unintended irony), and it consists of Peabody talking to his minister, the Reverend Amory S. T. Milbank, about the accumulated hang-ups of a lifetime. Or, I should say, the hang-ups of all the lifetimes of all his ancestors beginning with Increase Peabody, who landed at Plymouth in 1622, founded a bank, and was caught peeping at an Indian maiden bathing naked in a nearby stream. Thus Bradford establishes the twin themes which form Peabody's "complaint" and which, in a larger theological context of original sin, form the collective guilt of the Protestant Episcopal manchild: namely, his remorse over making so much money and his carnal yen for girls of a lower and therefore untouchable caste.

"Tell me, Reverend Milbank," Peabody asks the rector in a burst of self-revelation that may offend some readers with its frankness, "what is this compulsion that we have for banking? As early as nine years old I would lock myself in my room—three or four times a day—and do compound interest. Sometimes I even did it during dinner. Once I excused myself from the family table, saying I felt sick, and went into the bathroom and figured the compound interest on the Rockefeller estate at 4¼ percent for twenty years. My mother, who was a Lowell, kept knocking very politely on the door. 'What on earth are you doing in there for so long, Goody, dear?' she called. 'Please come out—your father wants

to read us all something from *The Wall Street Journal*.'
How could I tell her what I was doing? Or that I couldn't
stop doing it?"

It is an episode that recurs over and over, well into
Peabody's teens. The locale may change—it might be
the lavatory of the Buckley School, for instance, or
under the bath houses at the Piping Rock Club—but the
obsession is always the same, and one can only admire
Bradford's integrity for confronting such a long-hidden
taboo so openly. With this giant leap of the imagination
he has pushed the literature of Protestant adolescence
far beyond Penrod and the Hardy Boys.

Equally courageous is his handling of the novel's
other theme, the hitherto forbidden subject of Indian
sex. True, I was shocked at the first mention of it, when
Peabody comes right out and says, "Let's face it,
Dr. Milbank, I have a thing about Indian girls, especially
Iroquois," But then I realized that only by this very act
of spoken expiation—by moving out, as it were, beyond
guilt—could Peabody exorcise the buried fears and
fantasies that had made him psychologically impotent,
stunted by the Freudian dread of tribal castration.

Nor does he stop with mere words. Driven by the
need to find some meaning in his aberrant sexual bent,
he tracks down the diaries of his ancestors and finds
that the taint did not end with Increase Peabody, but
descended in a direct line through his son Cotton, his
grandson Enoch, and his great-grandsons Caleb and
Jonathan. No wonder Goodhue Peabody, Jr., the vessel
for three and a half centuries of bottled-up lechery,
decides to "get it out once and for all." And what an
uproarious romp it is, leading him to an Iroquois reservation where, one night in a tepee with six Indian girls
dressed only in beads, half blind with firewater and
desire, he gives himself to a bizarre form of the ancient
"potlatch" ceremony, emerging three days later with a

gigantic hangover but oddly purified. "I've had it with the Indian broads," he tells the Reverend Milbank in the rectory over tea.

Yet Bradford is too good a writer to let us off as easily as that. At the end we are left with the knowledge that Peabody's voyage through the dark night of the soul is but one of many that he will be called upon to make, and it is this rare insight into the human condition which raises the novel to grandeur. I, at least, found myself curiously moved by the possibilities of both pain and hope adumbrated in the final question that Peabody puts to the minister: "Say, do you think I've got any chance of making out with a Jewish girl?"

The Contributors

WOODY ALLEN, who is said to prefer writing casuals to writing movie scripts, lives in New York, when he is not somewhere else.

ROGER ANGELL is a writer and editor for the *New Yorker*. He lives in New York.

MICHAEL ARLEN writes both fiction and nonfiction for the *New Yorker*, for which he is also the television critic. He lives in New York.

DONALD BARTHELME, a regular contributor of fiction to the *New Yorker*, lives in New York.

HENRY BEARD is one of the founders of the *National Lampoon*. He lives and works in New York.

BURTON BERNSTEIN is a staff writer on the *New Yorker*. He lives in Connecticut.

MARSHALL BRICKMAN, like Woody Allen, writes both movies and casuals. He lives in New York.

GORDON COTLER, whose work sometimes appears under the name "Alex Gordon," lives in New York.

GERALD JONAS is a staff writer on the *New Yorker* and a science-fiction reviewer for the *New York Times*. He lives in New York.

GARRISON KEILLOR writes his fiction and lives his life in St. Paul, Minnesota.

CHARLES McGRATH and DANIEL MENAKER are both editors and writers for the *New Yorker* and live in New Jersey and New York, respectively.

THOMAS MEEHAN is currently most concerned with television and theatre, although casual-writing is his first love. He lives in Rockland County, New York.

MICHAEL O'DONOGHUE, an original contributor to the *National Lampoon*, now writes mainly for television. He lives in New York.

THE CONTRIBUTORS

MARK SINGER is a staff writer on the *New Yorker*. He lives in New York.

JAMES STEVENSON is an artist and writer for the *New Yorker*. He lives in Connecticut.

CALVIN TOMKINS, who is often confused with Calvin Trillin, is a staff writer on the *New Yorker*. He lives in Rockland County, New York.

CALVIN TRILLIN, who is often confused with Calvin Tomkins, is a staff writer on the *New Yorker*. He lives in New York.

GEORGE TROW is a staff writer on the *New Yorker*. He lives in New York.

JOHN UPDIKE writes his fiction, nonfiction, and poetry in Boston, Massachusetts.

ANDREW WARD writes for various magazines and lives in New Haven, Connecticut.

WILLIAM ZINSSER writes, teaches, and performs the duties of Master of Branford College at Yale University, in New Haven, Connecticut.